A Voter's Guide to *Homo politicanus*

How to Identify
Political Species
in the Wild

With an Introduction by Charles Darwin

Written and Illustrated by Shaktari Belew

HomoPoliticanus.com

DEDICATION

The overall structure of this book was inspired by the many people exploring theories and practices that offer new lenses through which to view voter options, policy decisions, and innovative approaches to all of humanity's complex issues.

To learn more, here are a few places to start
:

- **Permaculture Principles** - thinking tools for an era of change. (n.d.), from https://permacultureprinciples.com/
- **The Permaculture Research Institute**. (n.d.), from http://permaculturenews.org/
- **The Biomimicry Institute** – Inspiring Sustainable Innovation. (n.d.), from http://biomimicry.org/
- **Biomimicry 3.8**. (n.d.), from http://biomimicry.net/
- **Waters Foundation**. (n.d.), from http://watersfoundation.org/
- **Donella Meadows Institute** (n.d.), from http://donellameadows.org/

CONTENTS

FORWARD

You have the power to make this country and your future the way you want. But how do you know what you will get in a candidate?

They say a lot of things, and some do a lot of mud slinging. What kind of person are they really? What are their principles? How will they act in difficult situations? What decisions will they make that impact your life and your opportunities for peace, prosperity, education, and the lifestyle that you seek? What example will they set and promote for how people treat each other every day?

If you want a simple and easy path for obtaining answers to these questions, so that you can make an informed decision when you vote, you are in the right place! This book helps cut through the noise of consolidated, profit-based media so you can readily consider politicians **through the lens of a logical, evidence-driven, whole-systems specialist** - more interested in facts than sound bites, experience and depth of understanding over simplification, intelligence over clever manipulation, and (most of all), compassion over indifference. It is structured so you can easily go directly to specific issues important to you.

Politicians are a unique species of human and this book will not only help you select the right one for you, but also identify their heretofore unknown unique categorical name in the world of *Homo politicanus*.

Let's make your country, state, and community what YOU want it to be by exploring who these candidates really are and what they will do using the unique lens of *H. politicanus*.

So ... imagine if you will, that you are a specialist trained to spot helpful clues to species identification in the wild. **With field manual in hand and a sense of comedy, joy, and exploration in our hearts ... let's embark on this adventure together!**

INTRODUCTION

Welcome to the first
professional guide to
identifying variations of
the newly discovered
Homo politicanus!

Back in my day, identification of zoological specimens was usually
done through a combination of physical and ecological attributes.
But today DNA analysis allows for highly accurate identification,
and even the occasional new species discovery, as in this case.

Even so, *Homo politicanus*, can be a bit trickier to identify
accurately, as it tends to morph and blend into the local
population. And since we can't always utilize DNA analysis in the
field, our techniques must be all the more creative and rigorous.

To that end, I've gathered a team of top Taxonomists,
Evolutionary Biologists, Ecologists, and Zoologists from around
the world to develop this new identification guide.

Because we plan to release future updates as our knowledge of
the various *Homo politicanus* sub-species expands, please
contact us with any new or difficult to identify specimen data that
you discover in your field work.

We hope you enjoy learning this new methodology for
identification specific to this species. Hopefully, it will help you
find out which ones you have seen and perhaps even interacted
with during your ventures into democracy.

Charles Darwin

As long as there have been politicians, they have been the subject of jokes.

One of the penalties for refusing to participate in politics, is that you end up being governed by your inferiors.

PLATO, *the ancient Greek philosopher*

But recent DNA evidence has revealed them to be a distinct species, ***Homo politicanus***, new to the scientific community.

We have developed this Field Guide utilizing new scientific methodologies to create the first ever ***Homo politicanus* Species Database**.

Homo politicanus is a rather diverse species, indigenous to huge areas of planet Earth, though they tend to congregate in areas frequented by crowds of humans.

This book will concentrate on identifying the more common species found in the United States.

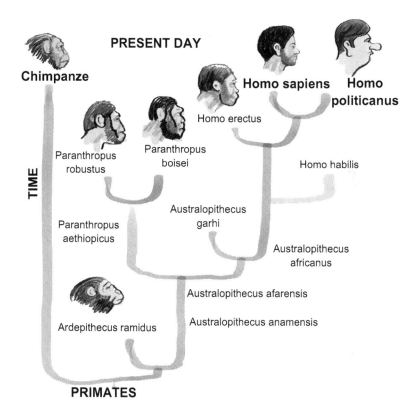

Even within a given Bioregion, the species shows immense variation in form and behavior.

It is believed that this wide range of diversity helps the species function effectively within their ecological niche.

In fact, studies have shown that when diversity diminishes, ecological balance can be lost due to congested thought processes, *over-consumption of available resources, and thoughtless, profit-driven environmental destruction.*

HOW TO USE THIS GUIDE

We've developed a handy process, consisting of steps and questions in several categories, to help ease identification.

Blah, blah, blah…

As you encounter a specimen in the wild, start with the chapter entitled **Observe and Interact**. Then move through the following chapters, each based on a specific category of inquiry. Feel free to skip from category to category until your sample specimen has been clearly identified.

We hope you enjoy your venture into the wonderful world of **Homo politicanus** field identification.

1. Observe and Interact

First, as you observe the subject in various situations, what do you notice?

Ask yourself...

- Where does the subject spend most of its time, and why?

- What excites this specimen?

- Based on its verbal communication, can you tell how it focuses its attention and why?

**Second, can you determine how it gains
its information?**

**Is it open to exploring
many, diverse sources?**

Does it listen
to diverse
constituents?

Does it
research
thoroughly?

Does it use
appropriate
senses?

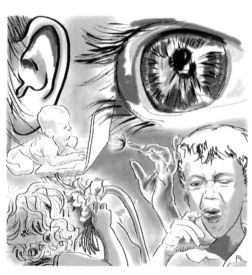

Does it
personally
witness
issues?

Does it
touch
those
affected?

Does it
make an
effort to
taste their
experience,
to walk in
their
shoes?

Is it willing to stretch into new ways of seeing?

Or does it primarily rely on a narrow field of
knowledge and experience?

Does the specimen adhere to certain ways of seeing or believing that impact the options it is willing to consider?

For example, does it see life as ...

"Survival of the Strongest"

Does it promote actions that teach "Might makes Right, " easily jumping to war and aggression as an automatic response to international issues?

Or do its actions show empathy, a preference for diplomacy, finding common ground, etc. BEFORE considering violence?

This can be obvious or extremely subtle. For example, whenever diplomacy is used, does this specimen complain that issues must be handled, "from a place of strength, not weakness"?
.
If so, this specimen could be using a very archaic and ineffective definition of STRENGTH. Similar to the stance of the school-yard BULLY, such boisterous bravado usually hides inner insecurity and fear. It is a stance of weakness, regardless of what it looks like on the surface.

Homo politicanus
learning more
effective ways to
confront (or stop
being) a bully.

Studies show that REAL STRENGTH often comes from CURIOSITY.* True curiosity comes with a desire to learn by being willing to LISTEN to all sides of an issue, to RESPECT all involved and their diverse points-of-view, and to focus on evidence-based FACTS. Those seeking actual solutions work with people and promote trust and community well-being over fear, reactionary measures, and future pain.

History shows that using these skills first leads to cultures that handle change well and produce adaptable solutions that lessen the likelihood of future unintended negative consequences. But it takes time and skill - much more than just using BIG sound bites and a BIG stick.

Example: An eastern (New York City) variety of **dominatus controlius x me-itis**. *WARNING: Almost never questions its assumptions, and rarely bothers with actual facts.*

If your specimen prefers "Might makes Right" solutions, feels most at home with **AUTHORITARIAN** attitudes, sees everything in life as a contest between "winners" and "losers", and is certain that its point-of-view is always the correct and only one, it may be from the more common Subspecies, **Dominatus controlius** -- a difficult sub-species to bring into ecological balance when its numbers get too extreme.

That is ... ***until they turn on each other.***

Another subspecies tends to see life as...

"Survival of the Collaborators"

Ask yourself:

Do this specimen's actions show a
preference for learning from diverse
points-of-view; using diplomacy and
respect; and finding common
ground?

If so, it is rare.

Most **Homo politicanus**, however, use a combination of the two.
Sadly, the choice between collaboration or domination is often
strongly impacted by simplistic corporate media reaction.

If it is open to exploring many points-of-view, embraces peaceful solutions before military ones, and is willing to listen to conflicting experiences by those directly impacted by its decisions, it may be from one of the rarest Subspecies: ***exploritatus openus***, who understands that all of these topics (below) are not separate, but interconnected.

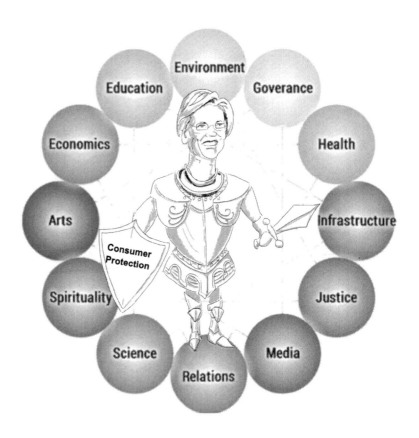

Example: An eastern (Massachusetts) variety of
exploritatus openus x accountabilitus

The opposite traits of **exploritatus openus** also exist, though usually as a trace DNA mixed in with more dominant subspecies. However, occasionally this subspecies shows itself strongly in certain hybrids.

You can tell it by its closed mind. It is always certain that its perception is the ONLY correct one, and thinks it is on a mission to force that perception down everyone else's throat through highly restrictive, unjust, and undemocratic policies. It is called **zealot-itis**, and is usually associated with radical religious beliefs (regardless of the religion) - though it can express through non-religious beliefs too.

Beware of *zealot-itis*!

It is exceedingly dangerous and often finds extreme measures acceptable within its delusional mind.

Examples: Similar types of **zealot-itis** DNA expressing through two well known **Homo politicanus**

2. ENERGY

Effective & Efficient

Energy flows from thing to thing. Successful survival strategies for all Earth species depend on utilizing energy well. That is, **accomplishing as much as possible with the least amount of energy used.** This includes not just personal energy, but also the energy of others, of tools, and of systems used.

Effective
Did it actually accomplish the goal?

Efficient

	NO	**YES**
NO	*Yuck!*	*Wasteful, but doing some good.*
YES	*Fails, but at low cost.*	*Sweet Spot!*

Did it use as little energy & resources as possible?

Does this specimen maximize time and effort
by being both efficient and effective?

Personal Energy

Is this specimen a drain on the ecosystem, constantly spending energy focused on drama and fund-raising instead of substance and actually doing the job it is paid to do?

Personal Energy

Does it "Walk its Talk" or does it use deception, manipulation, and **energy** to seem one way (and divert attention), while spending additional energy actually doing something else?

Is this specimen willing to use actual data and logic when determining policies, or does it prefer some of the following strategies?

Do the following logic manipulations sound familiar?

Either/Or Fallacy: Framing the issue to make it appear that there is only one good and one bad option.
- "Either we kill them, or they will kill us!"

Straw Man: When a person simply ignores a person's actual position and substitutes a distorted, exaggerated or misrepresented version of that position, defeats the made-up version, and then claims victory.
- "Flint, MI needs to have its water pipes replaced in order to provide clean drinking water to its citizens."
- "Replacing the pipes will cost millions and involve state and federal government agencies. People who think Flint, MI citizens should have clean drinking water believe in big, intrusive government, and must be ignored."

Slippery Slope: If there is no causal connection between A, B, and C: argue that if we do A, then B will happen. If B happens, then C must surely follow. Therefore don't do A.
- "If we allow the government to do background checks on all gun sales, they will know who has guns. If they know who has guns, they will come for them."

Perfect Solution: Assumes that, since the proposed action will not solve all of the problem, it should be rejected. In a complex world, rarely do single perfect solutions exist.

- "Cutting Carbon emissions won't decrease Methane emissions. Therefore, it won't solve climate change."
- "Criminals don't follow gun laws, so there is no reason to have them."

Hasty Generalization: Generalizing a small sample of some population to the whole population. Example: A few welfare recipients have played the system. Therefore...

- "ALL welfare recipients are lazy moochers."

Appeal to Fear: Scare the audience with fearsome predictions of what "the other guy" will do if elected.

- If you don't elect me, you'll get a loser, who won't know how to stand up to (fill in the blank).

If it "Walks its Talk" then it is most likely from the subspecies ***accountabilitus***, which is extremely rare - especially if it has done so for decades. It's even more rare if it cleans up any messes it makes. **Note**: This sub-species is so rare, we can't find a pure example. However, DNA analysis shows a consistent presence.

EXAMPLE: This particular hybrid example is the most common, ***accountabilitus x openus exploritanus***, and hails from Vermont. However, he also shows definite signs of the rarer ***x resilientitus*** DNA.

- As Mayor, he revitalized the economy and worked collaboratively to find solutions to existing issues.

As an independent Senator and Congressman, who always had to form alliances to pass legislation, he learned to collaborate. He also found his effectiveness niche in passing Amendments, so many that one magazine dubbed him the "*Amendment King*."

- He received the VFW's 2015 Congressional Award, (since 1964 presented annually to the House or Senate member who made the most significant legislative contributions on behalf of veterans).
- As Chair of the Senate's Veteran Affairs committee during the 113th Congress (2013-2014), 13 of the committee's bills became law. That accomplishment was during the second *least productive* Congress in American history!

Energy of Others

Does the specimen value and appreciate the efforts of others?

Energy of Others

Does the specimen show compassion and genuine care for others?

EXAMPLE: A common east coast ***dominatus controlius x me-itis x twofacedus*** hybrid..

Energy of Tools

TOOLS can be defined as:
- Products and output,
- Processes (methods of production, etc.),
- or Systems (the entire lifecycle design and its interdependent relationships from beginning to end).

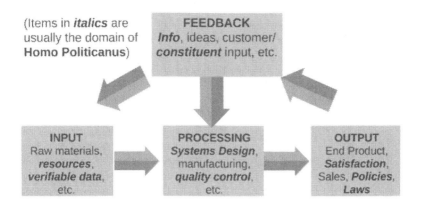

When you put it all together, you can see the entire lifecycle SYSTEM and all other systems it impacts. These can include communities, economics, healthcare, resource and environmental balance, jobs, and just about everything else in our interdependent, complex world.

Energy of Tools

Many variations of **Homo politicanus** use tools to further their goals. The tools they use, and how they choose to use them, can provide valuable insights into their behavior.

Does this specimen utilize only tools, regardless of their quality or impact on the ecosystem, that benefit its family and friends? If so, then it most likely is from the common Subspecies, **lobbyitus**.

NOTE: Because **lobbyitus** is so willing to accept bribes in exchange for favors, it usually is combined with **me-itis**, too.

Energy of Tools

Or does it seek out the most efficient, safe, and effective tools that benefit the entire ecosystem, not merely a select few? If so, perhaps this specimen is focused on "system resilience."

Resilience is defined as "an ability to recover from or adjust easily to misfortune or change."

The ability to understand **RESILIENCE** comes from a desire to understand the entire system over varying time frames, not merely a specific part or moment.

It requires the ability to see both macro and micro elements, and to step beyond temporary "quick fixes" that often lead to bigger problems in the future.

If your specimen seems to understand and promote Resilience among its constituents, it most likely comes from the rarest Subspecies of all, *resilientitus*.

Example: *resilientitus* subspecies from Delaware, on the US east coast

If not, it may be from the Subspecies **twofacedus**, one of the most common subspecies.

EXAMPLE: A **me-itis x twofacedus** with almost equal amounts of both. He originally hailed from the west coast (California) bioregion, but eventually became President.

3 YIELDS AND OUTCOMES

**What yields does this specimen produce?
Do they indicate its priorities?**

If Congress was Earth's doctor…

If you share the same ecosystem as this specimen, what benefits do YOU receive from its efforts?

- Are its efforts worthy of your support?
- Do its efforts support a high quality-of-life and a healthy community for ALL, or just a few?

If they benefit only a select few, it's probably *lobbyitus* again. **Lobbyitus** tends to only benefit the few who can afford its high-priced care and upkeep.

Note: *Single Payer eliminates the need for health insurance and can collectively bargain down the price of drugs for everyone.*

Example: This is a very rare example of the more common Washington DC area *lobbyitus x twofacedus*. That's because, in certain DNA combinations, (such as this example), they can demonstrate occasional **accountabilitus** behavior as well. Like many, this particular specimen has accomplished much good, too.

As it learns over time, this combination sometimes regrets previous votes and decisions. Hopefully that learning process constantly continues…

Another sub-species whose agenda is always personal, so it is rarely fighting for the best interests of all its constituents is ...

Me-itis.

Pure **me-itis** subspecies don't usually last long in politics because their yields are so obviously selfish. (However they often do great in business.) As a result, most **me-itis** are hybrids.

The Scientific Method   **The *Me-itis* Personal Agenda Method**

Me-itis usually mates with ***twofacedus***, producing a very common hybrid. You can tell if ***me-itis*** is present, however, by the outcome of its personal relationships. Do most people find this specimen difficult to get along with? If so, it is probably a ***me-itis*** hybrid, one of the most common subspecies, especially prevalent in Congressional habitats.

You can tell a ***me-itis x twofacedus*** hybrid because there is frequent flip-flopping on issues. But unlike those ***Homo politicanus*** who change their opinion as they learn more about the issues, (which is always beneficial to constituents), this hybrid flip-flops solely because it benefits its own personal goals.

EXAMPLE: This ***me-itis x twofacedus x zealot-itis*** hybrid is originally from Canada, though it eventually found its niche in Texas.

Lobbyitus and ***me-itis*** are all too willing to cast themselves as anything in order to scare necessary funding and votes from gullible constituents, while ignoring important issues.

Congressional
Caucus
Meeting

Determine if the specimen's actions are intended to actually **ACCOMPLISH** something that benefits and improves constituents' lives, or if they are meaningless gestures and a waste of time. Ask the following:

- What are the intended outcomes of any legislation?
- Are they clear and thoroughly understood?
- How would this specimen know if it succeeded?
- Are feedback mechanisms in place to see if the goal was actually accomplished?

Is the specimen open to **NEW IDEAS**, even if they could potentially undermine the status quo yet yield greater success for all?

Example:
A hybrid ***openus exploritanus x accountabilitus*** from the east coast known as FDR, surrounded by the innovative programs of the New Deal

As FDR exemplifies, those who seek to serve ALL within the ecosystem - and therefore eagerly seek solutions that work for all stakeholders (all who have a stake in the outcome) - are more likely a hybrid of ***resilientitus, accountablitus***, or ***exploritatus openus***. (Sadly, he did leave some constituents out. But we can learn from and improve upon his example of taking a whole-systems approach.)

36

4 FEEDBACK

Is the subject focused only on "quick fixes" while ignoring long-term, unintended negative outcomes; or is it serious about finding *actual solutions* to existing (and future) problems?

Is this subject open to developing feedback to improve its promoted ideas and solutions over time?

(Many complex problems don't show up for awhile, so it's important to include short and long-term feedback results when making that determination.)

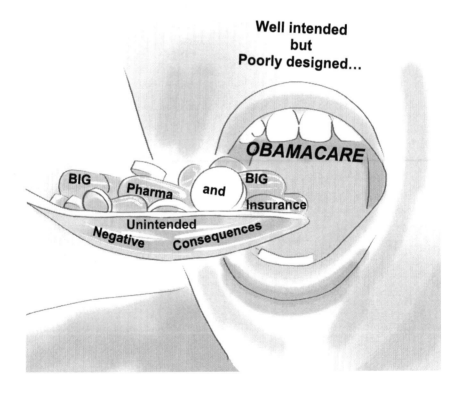

If your specimen is not willing to look at feedback & use basic logic regarding the design of our systems, most likely NOTHING will change for the better.

What the public sees ...

Hi, can I help you?!

The public actually believes that we will honor our contract with them, even though they know *it's not* in our best interest! We fight them every way possible, and *STILL* they keep health insurance private and tied to work!

What a gold mine for us!

The USA is *still* way behind the times!

What the Industry sees ...

US HEALTHCARE RANK in OECD
(Out of 34 countries)

Cost per Person	Last. Over double the average.
Life Expectancy at Birth	26th. We are even 2 years less than the average.
Drug cost per Person	Last. Over double the average.

Does your specimen ignore such strong feedback?

If so, why?

39

If your specimen receives strong feedback, especially the undesirable kind, is it willing to listen, learn, and act accordingly?

Example: A hybrid ***me-itis x twofacedus*** from the Great Lakes region of the USA.

See the Resource and Reference Section for More: Details, timeline, and links showing incredible lack of concern and action, even when the evidence of poisoned water was overwhelming. (The crisis reached its 2nd anniversary on April 25, 2016.)

There are many kinds of **FEEDBACK** (ways of determining if your goals were accomplished as intended).

For example: *Homo Politicanus* could focus on the question of whether its actions, policies, and legislation actually address the issue at hand. Yet few of them ever consider this vital question. Instead, many fall into the following feedback loop:

Really?

Typical Feedback

Lobbyist pays political bribes

H. politicanus **does Lobbyist's bidding**

The ***Homo politicanus*** species that are the most effective at accomplishing their goals use a feedback loop such as the following, which is rather rare. However, among those interested in actually accomplishing their intended goals (especially those thinking of whole-systems), it is common.

Rare Political Feedback

3. Homo politicanus learns, and supports adjusting the policy until the issue is solved. As conditions change over time, then appropriate changes are also made, repeating this cycle again.

1. Policy and legislation attempts to address an issue.

*NOTE: If **Homo politicanus** truly makes solving issues the highest priority, it resists the urge to attach unrelated "pork" provisions onto any legislation, to ensure transparency and passage of needed improvements,.*

2. Multiple feedback loops are designed and monitored to see if the policy fails to address the issue over time. Feedback sources include constituents, scientists, big data, etc.

Much better!

If re-election is the only determining factor for "success," then the subject probably is a **me-itis** subspecies of some kind.

However, if focused on developing proven legislation and policies (with accompanying feedback loops over varying time frames to determine success), then the specimen is more likely an **accountabilitus** subspecies.

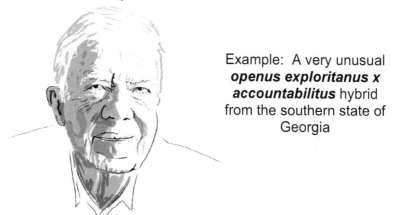

Example: A very unusual **openus exploritanus x accountabilitus** hybrid from the southern state of Georgia

"President Jimmy Carter had an unusual ability to think in feedback terms and to make feedback policies...

He suggested, at a time when oil imports were soaring, that there be a tax on gasoline proportional to the fraction of U.S. oil consumption that had to be imported. If imports continued to rise the tax would rise, until it suppressed demand and brought forth substitutes and reduced imports. If imports fell to zero, the tax would fall to zero. The tax never got passed.

Carter was also trying to deal with a flood of illegal immigrants from Mexico. He suggested that nothing could be done about that immigration as long as there was a great gap in opportunity and living standards between the U.S. and Mexico. Rather than spending money on border guards and barriers, he said, we should spend money helping to build the Mexican economy, and we should continue to do so until the immigration stopped. That never happened either."

5 SELF-REGULATION

Self-regulation can be seen as setting boundaries.

- The ability to control impulses and *stop doing something*.
- The ability to *do something undesired*, if necessary.

Example: A ***dominatus controlius x me-itis*** from the New York bioregion.

Is the specimen willing to question its own assumptions and to see through a different lens?

- What is the specimen willing to do or say, and what is it NOT?

- Are there lines it will not cross?

- Is it *logically* and *ethically* consistent?

When there is a conflict between desired outcomes, what does this specimen do?

- How does it prioritize what it is willing to fight for and what it is willing to ignore?
- How can you know? *
- Is it transparent about this?

Peace on Earth Goodwill To Men

Weapons for sale. Buy from the world's top supplier!

* If the public record does not reveal these answers, consider blogging, writing letters to the editor, participating in a Town Hall meeting with the specimen, etc. to make sure this becomes public knowledge.

Are the specimen's morals opportunistic or clear and consistent?
- How do you determine this?
- How does the *specimen* determine this?

In answer to all these questions, if the specimen deliberately questions its underlying assumptions, perceptual filters, and consistency, while also being transparent, then it is most likely some kind of hybrid of **resilientitus**, **accountablitus**, or **exploritatus openus**.

Though we have yet to find one, this close example seems to understand war and to be able to learn from the past.

"Every gun that is fired, every warship launched, every rocket fired, signifies, in the final sense, a theft from those who hunger and are not fed, those who are cold and are not clothed. The world in arms is not spending money alone. It is spending the sweat of its laborers, the genius of its scientists, the hopes of its children."

"Good judgment seeks balance and progress; lack of it eventually finds imbalance and frustration."

"May we never confuse honest dissent with disloyal subversion... Peace and justice are two sides of the same coin."

"Though force can protect in emergency, only justice, fairness, consideration and cooperation can finally lead men to the dawn of eternal peace.

"This conjunction of an immense military establishment and a large arms industry is new in the American experience. The total influence -- economic, political, even spiritual -- is felt in every city, every State house, every office of the Federal government. We recognize the imperative need for this development. Yet we must not fail to comprehend its grave implications. Our toil, resources and livelihood are all involved; so is the very structure of our society.

"I hate war as only a soldier who has lived it can, only as one who has seen its brutality, its futility, its stupidity."

"In the councils of government, we must guard against the acquisition of unwarranted influence, whether sought or unsought, by the military-industrial complex. The potential for the disastrous rise of misplaced power exists and will persist."

Example: President Eisenhower, an unusual **exploritatus openus x accountabilitus** hybrid with a military background who questioned assumptions. This specimen was native to the Kansas bioregion.

If you come across the extremely rare **resilientitus x accountabilitus x exploritatus openus** hybrid, handle it with care! **Do everything you can to create the necessary environment to help it multiply quickly!**

If your specimen fails to Self-Regulate, focuses on image over substance, or constantly seeks the quickest solution without concern for consequences, it is most likely a me-itis with a large amount of **lobbyitus** and **dominatus controlius** DNA mixed in.

Although each President and Governor swears to uphold the laws and Constitution, some have difficulty self-regulating themselves, legally and ethically. Here's an example:

Example: A western variety of **me-itis x lobbyitus x dominatus controlius**, mythologized by many as a hero. His rigid belief in HIS version of economics, regardless of contrary evidence, may indicate some **zealot-itis** DNA as well.

Questionable Ethics and Crimes:
1. **Throwing mental patients onto the streets**, resulting loss of 40,000 mental health beds and making approx. 125,000-300,000 homeless.
2. **Supporting and creating Islamic terrorists**, including the Mujahideen, Taliban, and Al-Qaeda. Before Reagan, Afghanistan was a democratic republic with improvements in women's rights and education.
3. **Involvement With McCarthyism**.
4. **Deregulating the banking industry and then rigging HUD** housing bids in favor of campaign contributors.
5. **Created the secret Office of Public Diplomacy (OPD)** to spread propaganda for the purpose of manipulating politics and media in South America by planting fake news stories. It was discovered by the Comptroller General—a Republican appointee—in September 1987 and declared illegal.
6. In first 3 years as President, over 20 high-ranking EPA employees were removed from their positions and in some cases imprisoned. Perhaps the most roundly illegal of these scandals was a scheme to fix elections with taxpayer money, otherwise known as "**Sewergate**."
7. **Selling illegal arms to Iran. (Part of Iran-Contra.)**
8. **Opposed the Civil Rights Act of 1964, the Voting Rights Act of 1965, and the Fair Housing Act of 1968.** Then when President, he supported apartheid in South Africa and vetoed the Comprehensive Anti-Apartheid Act.
9. The Reagan Administration and the CIA hatched a plan to **conspire with the Contras to smuggle cocaine** from South America into the United States.
10. **Supported South American Terrorists and Genocide.**

If your specimen fails to Self-Regulate by seeing everything as a personal bribery opportunity, then it probably carries a large amount of **me-itis** DNA.

Example: A **me-itis x lobbyitus** from Illinois now serving a 14-year prison term.

Former Governor Rod Blagojevich was found guilty on federal corruption charges (regarding the filling of President Obama's vacant Senate seat and more).

6 RESOURCES & SERVICES

How does this specimen see the role of humans on Earth?

Illustration inspired by a brilliant painting by Bea Jackson (http://beagifted.deviantart.com/ and http://beagifted.com/)

Does it have a core belief that the planet is here to exploit for human benefit only?

Or does it see the planet as a complex web of diverse life that must be honored and kept in **balance** in order for all species (including humans) to thrive?

Consumer vs. Human

Illustration inspired by a cartoon by Bradford Veley (brad@bradveley.com)

Stakeholders vs. Profit

Does it willingly collaborate with ALL stakeholders, especially those immediately affected by any possible decision?

Macro vs. Micro

Does the specimen make a point of looking at both the macro and micro potential outcomes of policies and decisions it makes, or does it focus only on the next election?

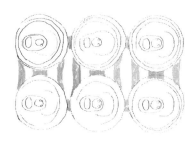

Now with easy plastic holder!

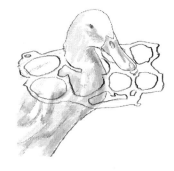

Now with easy plastic holder!

Now with easy plastic holder!

Now with easy plastic holder!

Balance vs. Exploitation

Can it recognize the ways in which every part of the eco-system (even the smallest) supports a healthy and balanced life for all?

Or does it adhere to the belief that only those with money and power actually DO anything meaningful?

Very Difficult Life

Very Comfortable Life
(Also made decisions that poisoned the environment to grow cotton, the oceans to transport, etc.

When designing a system (like Trade Agreements, for example), most **Homo politicanus** rarely take the time to fully understand the function and its impact.

~Donella Meadows
Thinking In Systems

"The *least* obvious part of the system, its function or purpose, is often the *most* crucial determinant of the system's behavior."

Is the specimen willing to take a WHOLE-SYSTEMS approach to issues?

"The bounded rationality (Narrow Perception) of each actor in a system may not lead to decisions that further the welfare of the system as a whole."
~Donella Meadows

Systems Thinking is a lens or Perceptual Filter that allows you to see things as parts of a whole. It focuses not only on elements, but also the RELATIONSHIPS between those elements. A Systems Thinking lens helps us realize that we live and participate in ever-changing, complex systems. In fact, that's a great description of EARTH!

It involves seeing things as they interact and change OVER TIME

It includes some basic understandings:

- Everything is connected.
- Like ripple effects in water, whatever you do impacts many things.
- As much as we'd like to find simple solutions or "quick fixes," they don't really exist in complex systems.
- Every solution usually creates new problems. The goal is to find solutions that don't also create unintended NEGATIVE consequences.
- To monitor the effectiveness of solutions, feedback mechanisms must be designed into the "solutions" from the start, and then subsequently monitored over time.
- Diversity in systems increases resilience.
- The simplest and most effective solutions are found at key leverage points.
- Nature is our best teacher.

Anyone, even **Homo politicanus**, can learn to think in systems quite easily.

In fact, many schools now include Systems Thinking lessons for students from Kindergarten on up.

The following pages show how easy it can be...

A specimen exhibiting a
WHOLE-SYSTEMS
approach will do the following:

Learn by observing patterns, trends, and how systems change OVER TIME.

Identify the circular nature of complex systems and their relationships.

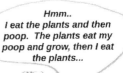

Recognize that a system's STRUCTURE generates its behavior.

Seek to understand the BIG Picture.

Consider an issue fully and resist "Quick Fixes" and quick conclusions.

Explore Mental Models and test assumptions.

Recognize the impact of time delays in Cause & Effect Relationships.

Look for unintended consequences

Use the system's structure to find the best possible LEVERAGE POINTS of action.

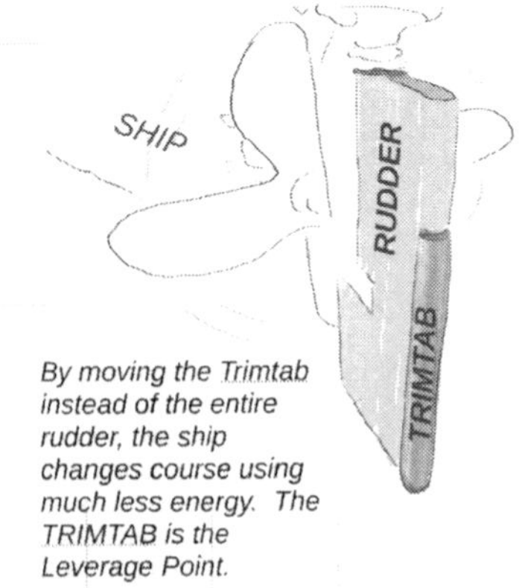

SHIP

RUDDER

TRIMTAB

By moving the Trimtab instead of the entire rudder, the ship changes course using much less energy. The TRIMTAB is the Leverage Point.

Change perspective to increase understanding.

I just see some sticks!

I see

4

sticks!

No, there's only **3**

(People have gone to war over similarly rigid perceptions.)

Check results and make needed changes to constantly improve toward the desired goal.

We went from people interactive, people-friendly towns...

To people-isolating, traffic-friendly towns

Consider short and long term consequences

Habits of a Systems Thinker text © 2015 Waters Foundation adapted with permission of the Waters Foundation; illustrations and content accompanying the illustrations express the opinions of the artist, not the Waters Foundation.
http://watersfoundation.org/systems-thinking/habits-of-a-systems-thinker/

Does this specimen seek out experts in science and leading-edge thinking?

Given that we've already created multiple dangerous issues:

1. **Water** - Huge ocean garbage islands (which means OUR food is ingesting OUR garbage), Ocean Acidification, Nitrogen and Phosphorus runoff pollution. Fresh water pollution/depletion....
2. **Land use, and land fill that pollutes** both land and water,
3. Multiple kinds of **air pollution and ozone depletion**.
4. Major **shifts in climate** causing flooding of coastal cities/islands worldwide, species migration (including humans) that upset the balance of (and even shift) ecosystems, etc.
5. Thousands of **untested chemicals interacting**,
6. **Fossil fuel, fracking**, and **nuclear** industry dangers
7. Massive **species die-off and biodiversity loss** ...
   just to name a few examples.

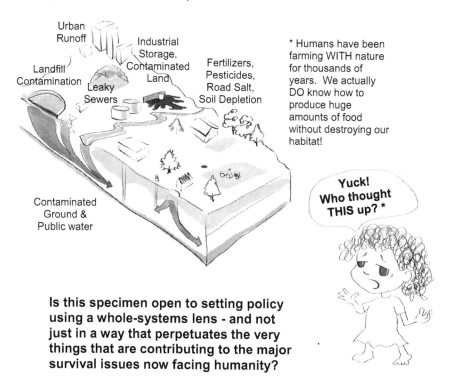

* Humans have been farming WITH nature for thousands of years. We actually DO know how to produce huge amounts of food without destroying our habitat!

Yuck! Who thought THIS up? *

Is this specimen open to setting policy using a whole-systems lens - and not just in a way that perpetuates the very things that are contributing to the major survival issues now facing humanity?

How does the USA rank internationally when addressing Environmental Issues?

According to their website, "The Environmental Performance Index (EPI) ranks countries' performance on high-priority environmental issues in two areas:
* protection of human health and
* protection of ecosystems."
It is based at Yale University.

With an overall score of 84.72 out of 100, the **USA ranked 26th out of 180 countries**, which means **25 are doing a better job than us**. Here's how the USA ranked in various:

INDICATOR	RANK	% 10-Year Change
Health Impacts	19	6.56
Air Quality	43	50.25
Water and Sanitation	22	0.34
Water Resources	42	-0.73
Agriculture	40	2.63
Forests	105	-0.43
Fisheries	84	-0.02
Biodiversity and Habitat	90	29.89
Climate and Energy	44	0

Clearly, we have more work to do!

What does that mean for Earth's non-human inhabitants?

"If half the animals died in London zoo next week it would be front page news... But that is happening in the great outdoors. This damage is not inevitable but a consequence of the way we choose to live."
~ Prof K. Norris, Zoological Soc. London's Dir of science

Cartoon by Tom Toro, created for the Center for Biological Diversity, used with permission from both.

"Let's raise it as one of our pack. That way we can be sure it grows up to be a fierce environmentalist."

Between 1970 and 2010 populations of mammals, birds, reptiles, amphibians, and fish around the globe dropped 52 percent, says the 2014 Living Planet Report by the World Wildlife Fund.

What does that mean for Earth's low-income inhabitants?
"High-income countries use five times the ecological resources of low-income countries, but low income countries are suffering the greatest ecosystem losses," said Keya Chatterjee, WWF's senior director of footprint. "In effect, wealthy nations are outsourcing resource depletion."

At the conclusion of the report, WWF recommends the following actions:
"We all – politicians, businesses and people – have an interest, and a responsibility, to act to ensure we protect what we all value: a healthy future for both people and nature." "The scale of the destruction highlighted in this report should be a wake-up call for us all."
~David Nussbaum, CE of WWF-UK

Humans as "WEEDS"

We have been brainwashed to think of WEEDS as unwanted nuisances. But as we learn more about nature, we are beginning to understand that there is no such thing, and that all plants serve a purpose in nature.

Weeds are actually PIONEER species, breaking up the rigidity of hard-packed, lifeless soil; shading (protecting) new life; and preparing the way for the next arrivals ...

How is this **Homo politicanus** applying that realization to our tendency to see certain humans as "weeds" or "waste?"

"A weed is a plant that has mastered every survival skill except for learning how to grow in rows." ~Doug Larson

Is the same true of perceived "human" weeds?

Is that why they bother so many?

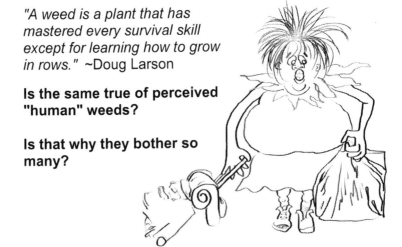

Is this *Homo politicanus* willing to produce no waste?

The concept of "WASTE" is unique to the human mind.

There is no such thing as "waste" in the REAL, natural world where everything is food for everything else.

Feedback loops clearly reveal the human assumption that anything can be "thrown away" doesn't work, and has resulted in immense devastation on our planet.

WASTE in GOVERNMENT

How is your specimen addressing the concept of waste in ALL areas of its career?

- Is it willing to use our government funds efficiently, effectively, and in a way that *maximizes* benefit for ALL?
- Does the specimen **WALK its TALK**?
- Does this specimen budget based on performance to ensure outcomes as intended?
- How about built-in **feedback loops** over varying time frames?
- Or does it hide unrelated expenses in bills just to benefit a few?
- Does it scream "WE NEED SMALLER GOVERNMENT!" while taking little responsibility to ensure that everything it does contributes to accountability and efficacy?

LINEAR vs CIRCULAR

Does the specimen attempt to understand and shift from the more familiar LINEAR to a more CIRCULAR way of thinking & designing?

Is it willing to explore the very real "circular economy" of every aspect of life, including ...

Materials Design	**Process Design**	**Systems Design**
raw and processed - Form: shape, surface, texture at all levels (macro - micro).	(methods of utilizing raw materials - operation & behavior)	(the overall total design - many forms & processes interacting) Including: • gathering materials, • processing them into the desired outcome, • after-use

Note: Often forgotten, but vitally important is
DESIGN FOR HUMAN BEHAVIOR.
Here's a rare example:
The Fun Theory – An annual contest "dedicated to the thought that something as simple as fun is the easiest way to change people's behavior for the better."

LINEAR vs CIRCULAR

- Raw materials & Waste
- Competition
- Cult of the Individual
- Added Value
- Standardization
- DownCycling

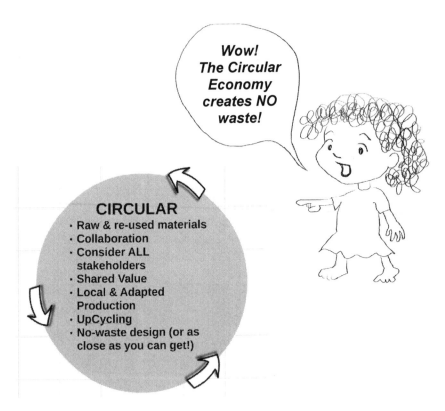

Wow! The Circular Economy creates NO waste!

CIRCULAR
- Raw & re-used materials
- Collaboration
- Consider ALL stakeholders
- Shared Value
- Local & Adapted Production
- UpCycling
- No-waste design (or as close as you can get!)

BIOMIMICRY
"Life creates conditions conducive to Life"

Biomimicry is the practice of applying lessons from nature to the invention of healthier, more sustainable technologies for people.

It is a CONSCIOUS EMULATION of life's genius. That is:

- **"Conscious"** being intentional
- **"Emulation"** learning from living things to apply essential patterns or principles within a strategy, rather than directly copy it, to solve human challenges.
- **"Life's genius"** recognizing that life has arrived at well-adapted solutions that have stood the test of time, within the constraints of a planet with finite resources.

10 of Nature's Unifying Patterns

1. Nature uses only the energy it needs and relies on freely available energy.
2. Nature recycles all materials.
3. Nature is resilient to disturbances.
4. Nature optimizes rather than maximizes.
5. Nature rewards cooperation.
6. Nature runs on information.
7. Nature uses chemistry and materials that are safe for living beings.
8. Nature builds using abundant resources, incorporating rare resources only sparingly.
9. Nature is locally attuned and responsive.
10. Nature uses shape to determine functionality.

Here are some of their insights into how Nature works

Because it requires expertise in a variety of fields, Biomimicry is always an interdisciplinary collaborative design process, tapping the genius of scientific, business, marketing, and design experts - whatever expertise is necessary to the chosen task - while simultaneously eliminating blind spots.

Unlike traditional Heat-Beat-Treat technologies, Biomimicry:
- Uses few, if any, toxins
- Uses ambient (local and body) heat
- Flows-with instead of dominates-over nature
- Is compatible with Earth's living systems

69

Examples of BIOMIMICRY:

SHARKLET: Imagine an anti-microbial finish on public surfaces, allowing the spread of illness to diminish significantly. That's the aim of Sharklet, a covering that mimics the nanobumps of sharkskin, shedding bacteria without the use of harmful chemicals. *More: http://sharklet.com/*

ORNILUX GLASS: Creating glass windows that birds can see - even though they seem clear to us. Humans do not perceive UV light, but birds do. Inspiration came when scientists noticed that birds avoid spider webs. They theorized that spiders might use UV reflective strands of silk in their webs so that birds would be able to avoid a collision, thus allowing the spider to preserve its ability to capture prey. So far, tests show great promise in reducing bird deaths.
MORE: http://www.ornilux.com/index.html

Finally, how does the subject define RESPONSIBILITY and ACCOUNTABILITY?

- Is it willing to see **RESPONSIBILITY** beyond merely keeping to its agreements?
- Is **ACCOUNTABILITY** merely obeying orders? Or is it more?
- Does being **RESPONSIBLE** and **ACCOUNTABLE** include the repercussions of decisions and policies over time?
- Does it include handling unintended negative consequences? If so, then it is likely a hybrid of *resilientitus, accountablitus*, or *exploritatus openus*.

Below, we see one of the growing number of *Homo politicanus* dedicated to a healthy environment. Here are some of Congressman Waxman's accomplishments:

- There is no EPA regulation of CO_2 without Waxman.
- Water is safer because of amendments he helped pass in the 80s and 90s.
- Waxman has been a leader for years in comprehensive climate legislation.
- He exposed the Bush Administration's war on climate science.
- He helped negotiate a compromise in 1994 that kept more pesticides out of foods.
- The auto industry pollutes less and makes more efficient cars thanks to his work.
- Waxman helped form the Safe Climate Caucus.
- Waxman also advocates for the Lead Contamination Control Act

Example: A rare decades-long environmentally-focused *exploritatus openus x accountabilitus x resilientitus* hybrid from the west coast in California

Here are a few more examples from both parties ...

Senator Barbara Boxer, California: She chaired the U.S. Senate Environment and Public Works Committee and cosponsored/coauthored many bills. Member: Senate Oceans Caucus

Governor Arnold Schwarzenegger, California: While in office, made California a global leader on climate change.

Rep. Raul Grijalva, Arizona: Environmental caucus memberships (4) and elected Ranking Member of the House Natural Resources Committee.

Mayor Greg Nickels, Seattle When the Kyoto Protocol became law for the 141 countries that have ratified it, Nickels launched the U.S. Mayors Climate Protection Agreement to advance the goals of the Kyoto Protocol through leadership and action. By 2014, 1060 mayors had signed on.

A few rare **Homo politicanus** are bucking the system and calling for bi-partisan action to address climate change. They have co-sponsored Chris Gibson's (R-NY) Resolution (**H. Res 424**).

Gibson's resolution could represent a major breakthrough among Republicans and offers the hope that Congress can soon work toward enacting bipartisan solutions.

The resolution states, *"Resolved, That the House of Representatives commits to working constructively, using our tradition of American ingenuity, innovation, and exceptionalism, to create and support economically viable, and broadly supported private and public solutions to study and address the causes and effects of measured changes to our global and regional climates, including mitigation efforts and efforts to balance human activities that have been found to have an impact."*

Those few brave Republican **Homo politicanus** so far include:

- Rep. Chris Gibson (NY-19)
- Rep. Ryan Costello (PA-06)
- Rep. Carlos Curbello (FL-26)
- Rep. Bob Dold (IL-10)
- Rep. Mike Fitzpatrick (PA-8)
- Rep. Richard Hanna (NY-22)
- Rep. Patrick Meehan (PA-7)
- Rep. David Reichert (WA-7)
- Rep. Ileana Ros-Lehtinen (FL-27)
- Rep. Elise Stefanik (NY-21)
- Rep. Frank LoBiondo (NJ-2)

EXAMPLE: A rare GOP **openus exploritanus** hybrid. This one is from New York.

Those ***Homo politicanus*** who actively fight against the environment are likely a hybrid of ***lobbyitus***, ***dominatus controlius***, and ***twofacedus***. Often, quite a bit of ***me-itis*** is also mixed in.

There is often a coven of them working together to brew up something in Congress while valiantly ignoring science, logic, and verifiable data.

When adults fail, sometimes children lead the way:
Like the children currently suing the federal government for not upholding the Public Trust Doctrine, which states that "it is the duty of the government to protect the natural resources that are essential for our collective survival and prosperity." Specifically, so far, they have won two court cases seeking "the legal right to a healthy atmosphere and stable climate."

For details, see: http://ourchildrenstrust.org/Legal

7 DIVERSITY

In what systems does this specimen dwell?

To what systems is it blind?

Ask yourself...

Is this specimen willing to consult diverse constituents, or merely those who agree with its beliefs and policies?

Does the subject actually LISTEN to those diverse voices? If so, does it listen for ***understanding*** or merely to refute what is said, and prove ITS point?

What voice does it most value? Why?

Without being willing to listen carefully to diverse constituents, **Homo politicanus** will most likely always perceive just what those in its own comfort zone (usual habitat) perceive, thus remaining blind to much of reality.

But there's an even more important reason to listen to diverse voices ... to LEARN from them.

Nature usually develops the greatest creative solutions to survival challenges at the edges of ecosystems.

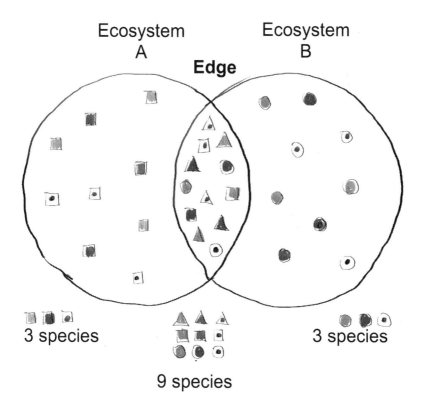

For example, where wetlands meet the meadow, or the meadow meets the forest. Those are the areas in which evolution provides highly creative solutions utilizing the combined offerings of both types of ecosystems and their diverse inhabitants.

Just as edge species tend to develop greater adaptability, the same is true regarding creative *ideas* and *innovative solutions.*

- *Valuing and learning from diverse ways of thinking, seeing, and experiencing benefits us all and helps eliminate blind spots.*

- *Valuing those who live and dance on the* **edges** *of our systems and whose ways of seeing, thinking, and being differ from the norm; provides us with new insights and propels us into greater creativity.*

So instead of making others wrong or dismissing them as "useless, kooks, or moochers," ask yourself ...

What can I learn here?

Similarly, if your specimen is only surrounded with like-minded people and those who experience the unique benefits of power and money, **how will it perceive *problems* facing the masses as well as possible creative *solutions* sourced from the majority** who experience significantly different ways of living, being, and thinking?

And if only those who dwell in the most privileged environments are given the task of designing systems that impact us all (economic, educational, medical, trade, even innovative products, etc.) then they will most likely design for what is personally familiar in their world, that benefits *them*, and promotes their own comfort and ease.

Homo politicanus could serve ALL its constituents better by valuing and learning from those who dwell in the marginal edges of our systems, ways of seeing, and thinking.

Diversity also includes considering ALL stakeholders - not just human - who are affected by policies and legislation.

This is especially important as we learn that humans are not separate from the environment, but part of it. Whatever we do negatively to it harms us as well.

Sadly, those negative unintended consequences ALWAYS come back to bite us.

Why not consider ALL diverse affected parties BEFORE setting policies into action? This concept is encapsulated in the **PRECAUTIONARY PRINCIPLE**.

Simply put, the Precautionary Principle asks all who set policy, invent, market, construct, produce, etc., to first, (just like doctors), **"DO NO HARM."**

If this specimen is blind or disdainful to Edge-Dwellers, the unfamiliar, or even diverse points-of-view, it most likely is our old friend, the hybrid of **lobbyitus**, **twofacedus**, and **dominatus controlius** (with varying amounts of me-itis for good measure).

Example: A **dominatus controlius x me-itis** hybrid from S. Carolina

We've already got a raghead in the White House.

We don't need another raghead in the governor's mansion.

But in truth, a *Homo politicanus* who values and honors diversity is extremely rare, so any number of hybrid mixes could meet those criteria.

You've got to have that Sister Souljah moment with the party, where you have to be honest and call it what it is. You've got to be authentic. People are sophisticated enough to know when you're just full of B.S. It's a problem of authenticity. It is a problem of legitimacy when you're going to go speak to that community.

What do you say to them?

~Michael Steele,
Former chairperson of the Republican National Committee (RNC), responding to what he perceived as racist statements by candidates, with no official response from the party itself.

Example: A *Homo politicanus* hybrid from Maryland. (It is difficult to identify this hybrid, as he was in office for such a short time, and was very inclusive.) However, he displays aspects of *openus exploritanus* and perhaps even *accountabilitus*.

Those who truly value and use diversity echo the sentiments of this little girl...

8 WEALTH

Fixing a broken economic system by doing the same things that caused the system failure is like treating asbestos-caused cancer with more asbestos...

How does this specimen determine
NATIONAL ECONOMIC HEALTH?   GDP/GNP* or GPI or all 3?

Both the **Gross Domestic Product** (GDP) and the **Gross National Product** (GNP) are similar. They measure the size and strength of an economy, but are calculated and used in different ways. The **Genuine Progress Indicator** (GPI), looks at economic activity from the point of view of the *impact it has on the individual and society* - not the impact it has on a bank balance.

The biggest difference between the two is how they classify **costs** and **benefits**. For instance:

CRIME:
- **GDP/GNP** counts this as a benefit because it gives rise to property repairs, legal and medical fees etc.;
- **GPI** counts it as a cost because it damages people's lives and leads to stress.

VOLUNTEER WORK & EDUCATION:
- **GDP/GNP** totally ignores these because no money changes hands;
- **GPI** values both as a benefit for a growing economy.

RESOURCES & POLLUTION:
- **GDP/GNP** counts both of these as an income, pollution twice over (once for creation and once for cleanup!);
- **GPI** counts both as costs.

*GDP = consumption + investment + (government spending) + (exports − imports).

*GNP = GDP + NR (Net income inflow from assets abroad or Net Income Receipts) - NP (Net payment outflow to foreign assets).

So under the **GPI these are good** for the economy:
- low crime rates,
- pursuing amateur interests
- education
- careful stewardship of the environment

Politicians usually encourage growth in the GDP/GNP. Under **GDP/GNP these are good** for the economy:
- high crime rates,
- spending all hours at your desk
- environmental damage
- disasters
- illness

As of 2014, only Vermont, Maryland, Washington and Hawai'i have passed state government initiatives to consider GPI.

Ask yourself ... WHAT BEHAVIOR does each measure encourage?

How does this specimen determine
NATIONAL ECONOMIC HEALTH?

Other useful International Measurements are the **GINI** Coefficient, **Palma** Ratio, and the **IHDI**, widely used as measurements of INEQUALITY ...

- The **Gini** is between 0, where everyone earns the same, and 1, where one person earns all the money.
- The **Palma** ratio is defined as the ratio of the richest 10% of the population's share of gross national income divided by the poorest 40%'s share.
- **Inequality-adjusted Human Development Index (IHDI)** - The IHDI attempts to take a more rounded view of a country, by not only calculating the achievements of a country on health, education and income, but also on the distribution of this achievements among its citizens. It does this by discounting each dimension's average value according to is level of inequality.

Example: A ***dominatus controlius x me-itis*** from the New York bioregion.

So how does the USA stand?

The **USA Gini**: With $63.5 trillion in total private wealth the US holds the largest amount of any country in the world. But that wealth is unevenly distributed, and nowhere is that more evident than in the U.S., which also has the largest wealth inequality gap of 55 countries studied, according to the report.*

The **USA Palma**: Ranked 44th out of 86 countries, well below every other developed society measured. It's one spot below Nigeria, which has some of the worst political corruption in the world. It is surrounded by countries that have experienced heavy political unrest in recent years.

The **USA IHDI** = Ranking .755, it is one of the top 5 losers along with Iran, Namibia, Botswana, and S. Korea. The United States has a -23 difference between its HDI and IHDI ranks, suggesting that inequality has a significant impact on actual human development gains.

85

How does this specimen define
PERSONAL "WEALTH?"
Is it only money and power? Or does it hold a deeper and
more complex concept of wealth?

Family, Friends,
Health, Community,
Social Connections

Investments,
Businesses, Real
Estate, etc.

Nature, Events,
Instinct, Culture,
Religion, etc.

**HUMAN
WEALTH**

YOU

**NATURAL
AND
SPIRITUAL
WEALTH**

**FINANCIAL
WEALTH**

**INTELLECTUAL
WEALTH**

Skills, Experience, Education, Training,
knowledge to provide others, etc.

**Does it include various kinds of
CAPITAL?**

Let's explore them...

Various Forms of Capital and Currency

CAPITAL	CURRENCY	COMPLEXING to...
Social	Connections	Relationships, influence
Financial	Money in the form of local, national, digital, complementary, coupons, etc.	Financial instruments, securities, etc.
Intellectual	Ideas, Knowledge	Words, images, creative property, innovation, etc.
Experiential	Action	Embodied experience, wisdom
Spiritual	Prayer, intention, faith	Belonging, wisdom
Cultural	Song, story, ritual	Community
Individual	Skills, physical & mental health	Shareable knowledge, ability
Natural	Non-renewables, renewables, eco-services & wisdom	Soil, living organisms, land, minerals, etc.
Built	Functional constructed infrastructure	Tools, buildings, roads, technology, etc.
Political	Power, goodwill, influence	Favors, donations, votes, attention

Soooo many kinds of Currency! WOW!

Does this specimen consider "The Commons" when making decisions?

DEFINITION: The Commons are often overlooked and taken for granted. They can be defined as what we share, without which we cannot thrive and survive. It includes creations of both nature and society that belong to all of us equally and should be maintained for future generations. To many, the inclusion of The Commons in decision making simply means using Common Sense.

TYPES: There are several types of Commons.** They include:

- **Social, cultural, and intellectual commons, which are all replenish-able resources.**
    - Indigenous culture and traditions, community support systems, neighborhoods, social connectedness, voluntary associations, labor relations, women and children's rights, family life, health, education, sacredness, religions, ethnicity, racial values, recreation, silence, creative works, languages, words, numbers, symbols, holidays, calendars, stores of human knowledge and wisdom, scientific knowledge, ethnobotanical knowledge, ideas, intellectual property, data, information, communication flows, airwaves, internet, free culture, sports, games, playgrounds, roads, streets, sidewalks, plazas, public spaces, national parks, historical sites, museums, libraries, universities, music, dance, arts, crafts, money, purchasing power
- **Solar, natural, and genetic commons, which may be either replenish-able or depletable.**
    - solar energy, wind energy, tides, water power, oceans, lakes, springs, streams, beaches, fisheries, agriculture, forests, wetlands, ecosystems, watersheds, aquifers, land, pastures, parks, gardens, plants, seeds, algae, topsoil, food crops, photosynthesis, pollination, DNA, life forms and species, living creatures
- **Material, or material commons, which are mainly depletable resources**
    - the elements, rocks, minerals, hydrocarbons, technological hardware, buildings, inorganic energy, atmosphere, ozone layer, stratosphere

KEY ROLES of The Commons Sector:*
- Assure sustenance of all
- Represent nature and future generations in the marketplace
- Nurture arts and sciences for their own sakes
- Promote diversity, community, and democracy

The Commons is awesome!

Does it understand the difference between **common**, **private**, and **public** goods (property)? There meanings have changed over time...

- **PRIVATE** goods are produced and sold by businesses to consumers
- **PUBLIC** goods are regulated by governments for their citizens
- **COMMON** goods are preserved or produced for the use of everyone

CARING FOR THE COMMONS entails many factors:
- It is an **act of personal commitment**, short and long-term, **for the benefit of all.**
- **It emphasizes relationships and balance**.
- **It steps beyond regulating**. It must be nurtured through cooperation, sharing, and caring for future generations.

SOLUTIONS based on consideration of The Commons include distinctive innovations and policies that remedy problems by helping people manage resources cooperatively and sustainably.

How does this specimen stack up?

How would you know?

ASK!

Does it consider **QUALITY OF LIFE INDICATORS** when making decisions?

Is this specimen aware of and committed to a high **Quality of Life** for ALL its constituents, or just a few? How do you know? Here's one such indicator...

OECD BETTER LIFE INDEX includes:

Personal Security
Culture & Leisure
Infrastructure and Services
Education
Income & Jobs

Civic Engagement
Work-Life Balance
Environmental Quality
Health
Housing Conditions

What can we learn from these studies to increase quality of life for all?

"In virtually every country, men are able to fit in valuable extra minutes of leisure each day while women spend more time doing unpaid housework." ~ 2015 Report

How did the USA rank?
2015 Work/Leisure:

- 11.3% of the US work 50 hours or more per week. We rank **26th out of all 36** nations surveyed. We work way more than most!
- The USA ranked even worse on Time Devoted to Leisure and Personal Care, **32nd out of 36**.

Wow, The USA works long hours!

Does this **Homo politicanus** use a narrow lens regarding entrepreneurial effort or does it see the bigger picture, making policies that acknowledge and strengthen ALL aspects of business success?

"There is nobody in this country who got rich on his own. Nobody. You built a factory out there -- good for you.

But I want to be clear. You moved your goods to market on the **roads** the rest of us paid for. You hired workers the rest of us paid to **educate**. You were safe in your factory because of **police** forces and **fire** forces that the rest of us paid for. You didn't have to worry that marauding bands would come and seize everything at your factory...

Now look. You built a factory and it turned into something terrific or a great idea -- God bless! Keep a big hunk of it. But part of the underlying social contract is you take a hunk of that and pay forward for the kid who comes along."

EXAMPLE: An **exploritatus openus** specimen, Senator Warren, who proposed and established the Consumer Financial Protection Bureau - an independent agency of the United States government responsible for consumer protection in the financial sector.

We stand on the shoulders of millions!

91

Does this *Homo politicanus* make the very common logical error of confusing *economic* systems with *governmental* systems?

For example, what some *Homo politicanus* call:

Democratic-Socialism is a democratic **GOVERNMENTAL** system very *friendly to Capitalism*. It is embraced by some of the most successful countries in the world today.

Capitalism is an **ECONOMIC** system.

They are NOT mutually exclusive, though many in the USA mistakenly think they are.

Here's an example: **Denmark**

- The form of democracy in Denmark advocates for policies that typically place the welfare of the PEOPLE above the "free" market (one that places the highest priority on profit, above people and environment).

- What are their policies? In general, they want to ensure that every person has access to housing, health care, education, meaningful employment, and transportation. They usually also support gender equality and tolerance of differences.

- Much of what Denmark does is generally defined as the center or center-left in the USA. The USA often uses similar policies under different names, like **Social Security** and **Medicare**.

Forbes ranked Denmark, in the top 6 of the "World's Best Countries for Business" for ten straight years & first for 6 of those years!.

Denmark, and most Scandinavian countries are consistently ranked the most progressive, happiest, and equal in the entire world. Forbes magazine places it on the top of its "best countries for business" list, while the USA has been slipping in its standing for six years.

In business, Denmark is a market-based economy. According to Forbes, Denmark excels in the categories of freedom and low corruption, and the regulatory climate is one of the world's most transparent and efficient.

According to Forbes, one of the keys to Denmark's pro-business climate is the flexible labor market known as "*flexicurity*," where companies have great flexibility to find the perfect employees, and citizens have a great government provided safety-blanket to find the perfect match for their talents, education, and creativity. As a result, the Danish workforce is among the most productive in Europe while maximizing happiness and efficiency.

What is "FREE" about the "Free Market"?

In a pure free market, buyers and sellers conduct their business without any government regulation, following the dictates of "supply and demand." Advocates believe the market balances automatically through the complexities of those supply/demand issues. They believe it fosters immense creativity throughout society. And at the **MICRO** (personal) level, there is evidence to back them up.

However, there is far more evidence, over time, that those same beliefs blind us to the real negative **MACRO** impacts of that same "free market." So…

It depends on which lens you look through…

At the **MACRO** level, (affecting ALL life on our planet) a totally "Free Market" cost is great, and creates the following undesired outcomes:

- Constant competition demands and rewards the **"survival of the fittest"** mentality embraced by both ***dominatus controlius*** and ***me-it is***, leading to policies that disregard the safety and well-being of both the general public and all planetary life, simply to increase bottom line profits for the few.
- **Wealth is defined narrowly and increasingly equals power.** It promotes policies that increase inequality, with a small percentage of society benefitting at the expense of everyone else. (But ultimately it hurts ALL life, even at the top.)
- **Economic (and therefore societal) stability is undermined as greed, pollution, and overproduction** cause the economy to have wild swings that hurt all but the few who are cushioned from danger.

Obviously, some governmental regulations are necessary to balance MICRO/MACRO concerns. The amount of regulation is a constant topic of debate that rarely focuses on MACRO outcomes. But that is finally changing, as exemplified by the diverse business regulations embraced around the world and their rates of success.

So in conclusion, if your specimen is okay with only a small percentage of humans experiencing wealth opportunity and a high quality of life, then it is most likely a hybrid containing quite a bit of **dominatus controlius**, **me-itis** and **lobbyitus**.

Rick Scott "was forced to resign as the head of a company that pled guilty to massive amounts of systematic fraud, including 14 felonies, leading to a historic $1.7 billion fine."
— Alex Sink in a May, 2010, press release, rated TRUE by Politifact.

OFFSHORE MONEY HAVENS

The Panama Papers:

https://panamapapers.icij.org/

EXAMPLE: A **dominatus controlius x me-itis x lobbyitus** hybrid from the Florida bioregion, who is one of the wealthiest **Homo politicanus** in the country. He made his millions as the CEO of a firm that paid Billions in what was called at the time, the "*largest health care fraud case in U.S. History.*"

9 DEMOCRACY

Does this specimen understand what it means to be a Democracy?
"Government BY the people, OF the people, and FOR the people."

We, the Corporations of the United States of America ...

It should say, "We the PEOPLE!"

Corporations ARE People, my friends!

EXAMPLE: An unusual *lobbyitus x me-itis* hybrid, with some *openus exploritanus* mixed in.

Does it understand the difference between human beings and corporations, and the negative consequences legally confusing the two can produce?

Does this specimen know and understand actual *verifiable* history (from diverse view points), not merely oft-repeated myths and sound-bites?

Does it understand the reason certain features were debated and ultimately included in our Constitution, and *the context of the times* that made those arguments pertinent then, (over 200 years ago); but perhaps not now?   Does it understand that certain words had different meanings then, and that **context matters**?

In the context of *today's* world, just what IS a **"Well Regulated Militia"**?

So-called "PATRIOT"	ARMY	ORIGINAL MILITIA
• Real guns & threats • Serves self interest • Dislikes all who don't agree • Adult • Believes government is the enemy • Chooses which laws to obey • Believes in NO regulations • White • Often Christian • Mostly Male	• Best weapons • Volunteers to risk life to serve all • Adult • Mostly Law abiding • Any politics • Often poor • Any race • Any religion • Any gender	• No automatic weapons • Volunteered to liberate and birth new nation • Any age • Believes democratic government is the answer • Followed and created laws • Any economic status • Mostly white • Any religion • Male

Team Malheur

Does it understand the gifts *and* limitations of ancient Athens (Greek) democracy?

What about other forms of historical democracy from which our country may have borrowed?

The Iroquois Nation?

"The Six Nations are a wise people. Let us harken to their council and teach our children to follow it."

~ Ben Franklin

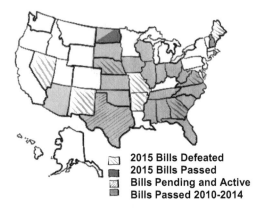

2015 Bills Defeated
2015 Bills Passed
Bills Pending and Active
Bills Passed 2010-2014

Does this specimen encourage ALL to vote, or does it do everything in its power to block potential voters who don't agree with its political agenda?

State legislatures have been considering hundreds of laws that could determine voters' access to the ballot. As of May 13, 2015, at least 113 bills that would restrict access to registration and voting had been introduced or carried over in 33 states. At least 464 bills that would enhance access to voting were introduced or carried over in 48 states plus the District of Columbia.

A mutually strong show of support for making the ballot accessible has not necessarily put voters ahead of where they have been in recent years, because **restrictive legislation continues to make it harder for citizens to participate.**

Some GOP members are tired of voter suppression. Rep. Jim Sensenbrenner (R-WI), introduced **The Voting Rights Act of 2015**. It has more than 100 co-sponsors, with 13 of them Republicans.

In a **democracy,** wouldn't you want to *ENCOURAGE VOTES* instead?

Does VOTER FRAUD actually happen?

Is this specimen aware of the efforts to stifle voters by fanning the flames of a *made-up* crime? Does it participate in such efforts? If so, why?

Only 31 Verifiable Cases Found...

"To put this in perspective, the 31 incidents below come in the context of general, primary, special, and municipal elections from 2000 through 2014. In general and primary elections alone, more than 1 billion ballots were cast in that period."

~ Professor Justin Levitt,
Loyola University Law School,
constitutional law. August 6, 2014

"Voter-impersonation fraud may be a subset of "misinformation." If so, it is by all accounts a tiny subset, a tiny problem, and a mere fig leaf for efforts to disenfranchise voters likely to vote for the political party that does not control the state government."

~ Conservative U.S. circuit judge,
Richard Posner. In his OCT 2014
ruling (Nos. 14-2058 & 14-2059).

"Out of 146 million registered voters, this is a ratio of one case of voter fraud for every 14.6 million eligible voters—more than a dozen times less likely than being struck by lightning."

~ Richard Sobel, "The High Cost of
'Free' Photo Voter Identification
Cards" 7 (Charles Hamilton Houston
Institute for Race & Justice, Harvard
Law School, June 2014)

Where does actual VOTER FRAUD happen?

When fighting for Voter ID Laws that limit access to the polls, TX Rep. Debbie *"Integrity"* Riddle herself was caught indulging in voter fraud on multiple occasions, voting for her absent colleagues in the House, thus silencing their voice, and by extension, the voices of anyone who's ever voted for them. (And she was not alone, this behavior takes place in many states.)

"Y'see, that's very important because **the very freedom of our nation is based on the integrity of our ballot box.** If things are so lax that fraudulent voting can occur, then that means your vote can be stolen. And when that's done, your voice is silenced."

(When caught on film stealing votes from other legislators...)

"Ahhh, We have a lot of amendments.

We don't have lunch breaks, dinner breaks, restroom breaks."

EXAMPLE: A not-so-rare Texas **twofacedus**.

Does it support the Electoral College or trust in the people to vote directly to determine their representation (as in many other democracies around the world)?

Concerns regarding the Electoral College:

- It can protect the interests of the minority, *and* give them too much influence at times.
- It promotes the two-party system. Good or bad?
- It can push a *minority winning candidate* over the top with the help of another candidate, Congress, or the Supreme Court:
  - In 1992 Clinton only got around 42 percent of the vote but won with Ross Perot's influence.
  - In 2000 Al Gore lost to George W. Bush, even though it seemed he won the popular vote.
- Unlike other methods (see next page), it precludes the possibility of a recount across the USA.
- It sometimes gets *less popular* candidates elected.
- ***Most importantly, it discourages voters as they feel their vote ultimately doesn't count.***

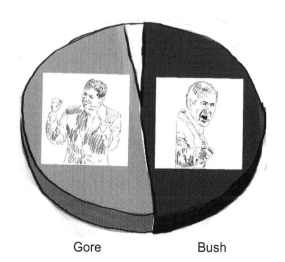

Gore   Bush

2000 Presidential Election - Popular Vote: *"Nobody can say for sure who might have won. A full, official recount of all votes statewide (Florida - where Bush's brother was governor) could have gone either way, but one was never conducted."*

101

Is it familiar with various forms of voting and the pros and cons of each?

For example, in our "**WINNER TAKES ALL**" current system:

- If two or more similar candidates, sharing policies favorable to the majority compete for the same job; it is too easy for a third candidate, representing the wishes of only a bit more than 33% of the people, to be declared the winner. Why? Because the similar candidates split the vote of the majority.
- Such a system promotes personality wars and negative campaigning.
- It also lessens the chances of substantive debates over important issues.

A different system of voting has been used in corporate shareholder meetings and other countries for years. It's called **INSTANT RUNOFF VOTING** or **RANKED CHOICE VOTING**, and it promotes a more policy-driven (not personality driven) campaign resulting in a more democratic outcome.

Does the specimen understand Tom Atlee's conclusion,
(based on Lao Tzu), that:

"Democracy is, in the end, about creating processes that allow people to empower themselves, not about Great Leaders saving the people."

Does it seek to understand other democracies and why they have decided to make any changes that differ from our approach?

2015 Top 10 Democracies
(Based on 2014 data)

1	Norway	6	Netherlands
2	Switzerland	7	Germany
3	Sweden	8	New Zealand
4	Finland	9	Ireland
5	Denmark	10	Belgium

...

16 USA

Does it see other democracies as lesser versions, even though the **USA ranks 16th and 19th** on democracy scales?

Is it curious *WHY* others are ranked higher than us?

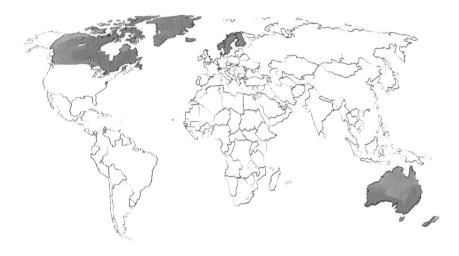

**The Economist Intelligence
Unit Democracy Index Map for 2014**

Countries by Rank:

1 Norway
2 Sweden
3 Iceland
4 New Zealand
5 Denmark
6 Switzerland
7 Canada
8 Finland
9 Australia
10 Netherlands
...
19 USA

Those who adhere to a more nuanced and context-driven system, usually have the ability to see macro patterns, and are more likely a hybrid that includes **openus exploritatus**. This is especially true if its willingness to understand democracy includes ALL forms (now and throughout history).

If it holds a very narrow definition of democracy, it is more likely a hybrid of **dominatus controlius**, **twofacedus**, or the very common **me-itis**. For example, does your specimen understand what the FIRST AMENDMENT of the CONSTITUTION means regarding separation of Church and State, and that it doesn't specify only certain religions (especially just its own)?

EXAMPLE: A **me-itis x twofacedus x zealot-itis** hybrid, originally from Canada. It eventually found its niche in Texas.

** **Cruz scores 100% by Americans United for the Separation of Church and State.** Scoring system for 2014: Ranges from **0%** (**supports** separation of church & state) to **100%** (**opposed** to separation of church & state). www.au.org

10 EQUALITY & EQUITY

EQUALITY assumes everyone starts at the same level.
EQUITY refers to the quality of justice, fairness,
impartiality, and even-handedness.

Equity and Equality can be seen in many ways...

EQUALITY   EQUITY

EQUALITY = SAMENESS.   EQUITY = FAIRNESS.
EQUALITY = QUANTITY.   EQUITY = QUALITY

Equity involves making sure people have access to the same opportunities, regardless of their differences, history, or physical barriers.

Equity must come first **before** Equality can be obtained.

In legislation, **EQUALITY** is often interpreted to mean rigidly "equal" treatment across the board.

For example, if a fine is levied, it is exactly the same for everyone. On the surface, that seems both equitable and fair, but it fails to take into consideration the **CONTEXT of each person's situation.**

A $1000 fine is nothing to a person of means. And because it is such a minor fee, it represents less of a deterrent. As a result, such systems can actually encourage negative behavior among the very wealthy.

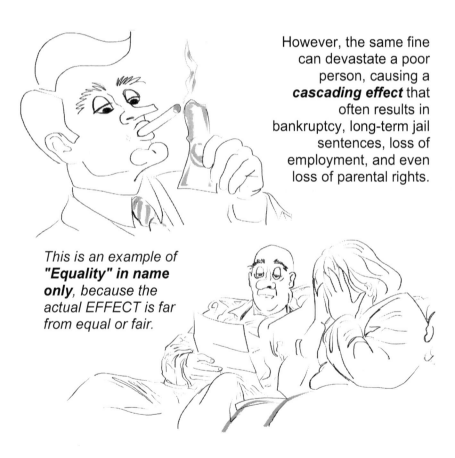

However, the same fine can devastate a poor person, causing a **cascading effect** that often results in bankruptcy, long-term jail sentences, loss of employment, and even loss of parental rights.

This is an example of **"Equality" in name only**, *because the actual EFFECT is far from equal or fair.*

If your specimen is for "**Equal Opportunity**," what *exactly* does that mean?

- Who is not included, under what circumstances, and why?
- Is the subject willing to utilize scientific data and feedback loops to determine if new or existing systems actually lead to greater or weaker opportunity for all?
- Is it willing to learn from others, including other countries?

This is the land of equal opportunity!

If you refuse to inherit millions, capitalize on connections, go to the best schools, be given starter money for your own companies, and hide profits overseas... that's *your own fault.*

- o Are these answers apparent in your specimen's proposed legislation and voting history?
- o Does it talk about it publicly?
- o Or does is automatically **assume** a level playing field for all?

There is a general assumption that Democracy = Equality and Fairness, and the US Constitution constantly refers to its importance.

So how does this specimen define Equality and Fairness?

Specimens rigidly adhering to penalties and systems that dismiss context in the name of pragmatism are usually from the sub-species ***dominatus controlius***, who tends to focus primarily on appearance and ignore substance, context, outcome facts, and common sense. This is especially true if the specimen adheres so strongly to a belief that nothing else matters, including **reality**.

* There is **NO evidence** either works as intended. They may even be *counter-productive*.

"*I was a big supporter of waterboarding.**

I was a big supporter of the enhanced interrogation techniques." *

EXAMPLE: An almost pure ***dominatus controlius x me-itis*** hybrid from Wyoming, who became VP of the USA.

NOTE: "Torture is defined by the UN Convention against Torture, which the US has signed, as "any act by which severe pain or suffering, whether physical or mental, is intentionally inflicted on a person" in order to get information. The US legal code defines torture as an action "specifically intended to inflict severe physical or mental pain or suffering", while the US Constitution bans "cruel and unusual punishment"."

Those who adhere to a more nuanced and context-driven system usually have the ability to see a bigger picture.

"Justice will not be served until those who are unaffected are as outraged as those who are."
~ Anonymous

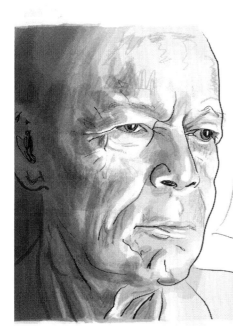

"Violence is black children going to school for 12 years and receiving 6 years' worth of education."

"There is a thin line between politics and theatricals."

"As legal slavery passed, we entered into a permanent period of unemployment and underemployment from which we have yet to emerge."

EXAMPLE: State Senator and Rep. Julian Bond, an ***openus exploritanus x accountabilitus*** hybrid from the southern bioregion of Georgia. He was famous for his work to create equality AND equity throughout his life.

11 CHANGE

EVERYTHING constantly changes. This applies to things AND their interdependent relationships. Instead of fighting change, why not DESIGN for it from the start?

Presenting: Murdoch-Adelson Productions

Sadly, most **Homo politicanus** think their job is to protect and maintain the status quo, especially if they feel it protects perceived benefits for those they most care about. (Yet this is an impossible task that always fights with the natural flow of change and adaptation.)

That is, unless …

Presenting: Koch Productions

... on a MACRO level, humanity is STUCK in an overall **pattern of behavior** that consistently yields the same negative results, with only the names or titles of the players changing over time...

Presenting: Empire-Monarchy Productions

Where do we stand at the MICRO Level?

REAL change requires a shift of perceptual lenses, or we are doomed to repeat past mistakes. Here's **one point-of-view** in the last 50 years ...

- **Women's movement** - Slow progress. Almost ALL countries are still unequal in pay, opportunity, education, and law. Laws to LIMIT women's choices about their bodies and lives have blossomed lately.
- **Work**: Work/Life balance - There was improvement in the USA for about 40 years where work hours were slowly replaced by additional leisure hours, but that ended in the 1970's. Many now work multiple jobs, just to survive.
- **Celebrity** - Our society still values celebrity/wealth over intelligence/creativity.
- **Education**: We've regressed to education aimed at test score outcomes. We no longer teach life skills and the questioning of assumptions, nor do we encourage creativity and innovative thinking. As a result, each generation becomes new cogs in the machinery of business and industry. Our lack of skills and understanding of nature has forced us to be "CONSUMERS" instead of CREATORS and HUMANS, so much so that few are even offended by the term.
- **Opportunity**: Opportunities available immediately during and after WW2, that helped build the middle class, have disappeared. Personal debt is much greater now, even just to get a university education. Medical bills can wipe out an entire family's progress. Structural racism and classism are still very alive.
- **Environment**: Industry still ruthlessly pillages whatever local resources it can, with rarely any attention on natural balance or whole-systems. Big Business frequently does so on an international scale, leaving the ruins for oft-abused locals to deal with.
- **Money still equals Power**: Thanks to recent Supreme Court rulings, the situation is out of control, as we citizens stand by and watch our democracy being destroyed before our eyes.
- **The "Other" is still made the enemy**:
  - Whoever is deemed "The OTHER," at the moment is verbally, systemically, and - increasingly - physically abused. Even Presidential candidates are jumping into the fray.
  - Systemic structural scapegoating and racism are still very evident and promoted by those in power. Most aren't even aware of the extent of the problem.
  - The poor are still made wrong and blamed for their lack of opportunity, or whatever it is deemed they "lack" at any given moment.

But what happens when we broaden our perception?

Where do we stand at the MACRO Level?

Let's begin with a global lens, using MACRO data.

It is easy to get caught up in the media reports and sound bites that use archaic terminology and misperception of the world. And, yes, we've had some set-backs. But if you broaden the scope of years, great progress has been accomplished. Let's learn from what has worked!

Luckily, statisticians like Hans Rosling of GAPMINDER have made great progress in showing us the FACTS of how much progress we have actually made over the last 200 years. HINT: It's huge, worldwide, in almost every category!

SOURCE: http://www.gapminder.org/

And beyond MACRO Level?

We can be so absorbed in our human-based ways of seeing the world, that we often forget a few realities of planet Earth...

Just as most fish never experience NOT-water, so they never question their assumptions of life or reality...

Only those who escape their *perceptual boundaries* can understand and consider new possibilities...

Beyond HUMAN Level?

We forget that most of what humans call "**REAL**" is all in their heads. None of it exists in the actual, REAL world of planet Earth. You know, that place we rely upon to survive.

Ask any astronaut upon returning to Earth. It is a profound realization that most of what we call "important" ONLY exists in the human mind...

- Earth has no political borders. All countries exist by agreement.
- In fact, everything in the human world exists by agreement, and can be changed whenever and however we desire. WE ARE MAKING IT ALL UP.
- There is no such thing as race.
- There is no such thing as WASTE.
- In the REAL world, everything eats everything else, but ONLY in balance, if all want to survive.
- We invented money and economies to benefit our ability to trade and complete large projects. We are free to invent it any way we choose.
- How we treat each other is also by agreement.
- If we want aggression, domination, and control, that is what we get. All we have to do is continue what humans have done for thousands of years with the exact same destructive results.
- If we truly want peace and prosperity, we must design our systems to produce that outcome; and we must learn to act that way in every aspect of life.
- If we want to solve the unintended negative consequences of our previous decisions, we must now collaborate globally - because the consequences are global and require that we work together.

The choice is OURS, each and every one of us...

How do we bridge the gap between MICRO and MACRO perceptions?

Let's start by acknowledging that some truth resides within ALL perceptions. Let's also acknowledge that even though facts and data exist, they can be perceived, interpreted, or ignored uniquely by each person.

Remember these guys...

Are we really willing to fight over perception?

Why not LEARN from it instead?

If we agree that we need to change our systems so that ALL benefit, and that to do so, we must humble ourselves enough to be WILLING to learn, and to see through new lenses. Then ...

HOW can we show HUMILITY regarding our own perceptions, and also RESPECT regarding those of others, and thereby grow and learn together?

- *See Resources for suggested tools for deeper and more connected communication:*

Just WHY do *Homo politicanus* (and humans) see Reality in so many different ways?

Studies show that THIS is how most *Homo politicanus* perceive...

My senses perceive stimulus from around me...

I interpret stimulus using my own unique body...

And my experiences, thoughts, and beliefs form **Perceptual Filters** that create blind spots.

I usually see what I want to see, and ignore the rest.

MY Reality:

Is constantly changing as I learn, grow, and experience life.

It develops similarly to a child's developmental psychology.

What and how I am willing to explore, changes as I learn to adapt to life's constant changes.

If I'm comfortable, I *rarely* change.

So ...

How do we DESIGN for change at Micro and Macro Levels?

Psychologists have been studying behavioral CHANGE for just a few decades. And while this area of study is relatively new, here are some of their accumulated insights...

Design for Change from the start. Joyce Hostyn has been a "Change Designer" for years, and offers her insights in her blog. Here are six things she and other change-designers suggest to remember:

- We learn through storytelling, and always have.
- How we frame our stories determines the outcome or take-away.
- We tend to take mental shortcuts when making decisions.
- We are poor at knowing what we want and therefore, why we do things.
- We tend to stick with our comfort zone of what we know, (or think we know.)
- We are shaped by experience. (Experience, along with beliefs and thought patterns create what I call, "Perceptual Filters" - what we allow ourselves to perceive.)

A recent study reveals that focusing on losing a reward rather than gaining one seems to motivate people (at least in this particular study), even if the financial results were ultimately exactly the same. **What can we learn from this?**

- If you really want to motivate people, find a way to make the end reward tangible now.
- Then make it clear the reward lessens as failure mounts.
- This seems to work better than dangling a grand reward at the end of a big effort. However, this experiment was in the context of staying fit. Can you imagine how we could re-imagine it in the context of other goals?

Perhaps most importantly, make doing the desired behavior FUN. The on-going *TheFunTheory.com* contest is dedicated to *"the thought that something as simple as fun is the easiest way to change people's behavior for the better."*
It has been a hit for years. Check it out!

- *See the Resource Section for Sources and More…*

How can we best discuss change with *Homo politicanus*?

Sarah Krasley develops tools for manufacturers to create more sustainable product and factory designs. Along with the other suggestions already mentioned, she suggests using METAPHORS about the outcome transformation and having fun while exploring and actualizing it. Here's one of her examples:

> When discussing how much energy ineffective or inefficient machines waste, (which can be boring for her audience), she uses the metaphor of cutting a tomato:

"... I drew the metaphor of trying to cut a tomato with a dull knife—it takes a lot more muscle to cut through the tomato skin and increases the chances that you will cut your finger in the process."

In all of her suggested approaches there is a "*beautiful humanism and a fun metaphor* that's easy to understand, punctuated with a 'We can do it!' call to action."

Perhaps the BEST use of Change Theories...

Although many change and communication theories can be extremely complex, they all seem to offer simple clues about how to **LISTEN FOR UNDERSTANDING** when discussing change (and any of the chapter topics in this book) with both voters and *Homo politicanus*.

So maybe the BEST QUESTIONS to ask ourselves are very simple:

> *How can I communicate in a way that honors each unique way of thinking and perceiving, so true communication can take place?*
>
> *And, again...   How can I make it FUN?*

Transferring awareness...

As you peruse the various categories for subspecies identification found within this book, we encourage you to consider how you, yourself, would answer these questions.

> *After all, if we demand accountability of Homo politicanus, shouldn't we ask the same of ourselves?*

We welcome your insights from the field and assistance in continually updating our *Homo politicanus* **Database of Subspecies and Hybrids.**

Thank you for your efforts on behalf of all of us!

Where do we go from here?

What are we left with?   Well, WE ...

- Still have the power of the **VOTE**.
- Still have the power of **numbers**.
- Still have the ability to **vote with our dollars**...
- Still have the ability to **learn** and to **LISTEN** to each other - especially diverse voices...
- Still have our own **voices**, our pens, technology, phones, social media, etc.
- Still have the power to make change, but ...

ONLY IF WE BOTHER.

Otherwise, the same old human patterns, (only now on a global scale), will continue.

We cannot afford to wait. Our lack of understanding whole-systems and our narrowly-focused designs now threaten the very existence of our species.

But here's the
good news,
it's *your* choice.

**Choose the world
you want, and ...**

Vote!

And why not have FUN, while you're at it!

Here are some ideas...

- Creative Flash-Mobs and Parties
  - Example: Gingerbread House Design Parties that include whole-systems, are place-based, and explore new ways of perceiving
  - Change-Perception Parties with colored sunglasses and other toys to literally experience what that feels like
- Explore new ideas and innovative solutions using tools like Open Space, Dynamic Facilitation, etc.
- Nature Journals
- Your own *Homo politicanus* Journal
- Consider whether perhaps YOU might harbor some *Homo politicanus* DNA, yourself!

Whatever excites you to your core about making a better world for all...

Do it!

Gratitude

The following people helped make this book possible:

Seth Belew
Marika Brobisky
Kesa Belew
Jeff Park
CJ Cuellar
Catherine Morris
Kimberly Shipman
Crystal Arnold
L. Benson
Nathan Bixby
Aliyah Bixby-Driesen
Tamarra Bartholomew
Chris Lopez
George A. Polisner
John De Graaf

*And the millions of open, creative thinkers
and doers who have come before,
constantly exploring and expanding the field
of the possible...*

References and Resources

PAGE	RESOURCE

11   *What is strength?*
- Kashdan, T. B. (2015, January 21). 10 Psychological Strengths, Including the Most Valuable 2. Retrieved May 19, 2016, from https://www.psychologytoday.com/blog/curious/201501/10-psychological-strengths-including-the-most-valuable-2

12   *Authoritarianism:*
- Williams, R. (20216, March 18). The Rise of Authoritarianism in America. Retrieved May 19, 2016, from https://www.psychologytoday.com/blog/wired-success/201603/the-rise-authoritarianism-in-america
- Taub, A. (2016, March 01). The rise of American authoritarianism. Retrieved May 19, 2016, from http://www.vox.com/2016/3/1/11127424/trump-authoritarianism

20-21   *Logical Fallacies*
- *Thinking Fallacies* , Professor John L. Cotton, Professor Justin Fisher, Professor Randall J. Scalise, Professor Scott Norris, and Professor Stephen Sekula, from their course: Physics 3333 / CFB 3333 / KNW 2333 The Scientific Method - Critical and Creative Thinking (Debunking Pseudoscience), Dedman College of Humanities and Sciences, Department of Physics, Southern Methodist University http://www.physics.smu.edu/pseudo/Fallacies/

22   *Sanders*:
- Jilani, Z. (2015, October 17). Bernie Gets It Done: Sanders' Record of Pushing Through Major Reforms Will Surprise You. Retrieved May 19, 2016, from http://www.alternet.org/election-2016/bernie-gets-it-done-sanders-record-pushing-through-major-reforms-will-surprise-you
- Taibbi, M. (2005, August 25). Inside the Horror Show That Is Congress. Retrieved May 19, 2016, from http://www.rollingstone.com/politics/news/inside-the-horror-show-that-is-congress-20050825?page=2

PAGE	RESOURCE

22
cont. ***Sanders*:**
- What Bernie Sanders Got Done in Washington: A Legislative Inventory. (2015, November 11). Retrieved May 19, 2016, from https://pplswar.wordpress.com/2015/11/11/what-bernie-sanders-got-done-in-washington-a-legislative-inventory/
- Inside Gov: Government Data Visualized, Presidential Candidates: Bernie Sanders", http://presidential-candidates.insidegov.com/l/35/Bernie-Sanders

24 ***Christie*:**
- Phelps, J. (2016, January 25). 'Want Me to Go Down There With a Mop?' Chris Christie Says About NJ Flooding Cleanup. Retrieved May 19, 2016, from http://abcnews.go.com/US/mop-chris-christie-nj-flooding-cleanup/story?id=36513815

26 ***Get Elected Get Your Family Rich***
- Malone, Clare,"Get Elected, Get Your Kids Rich: Washington Is Spoiled Rotten", Feb 27, 2014, The Daily Beast :, http://www.thedailybeast.com/articles/2014/02/27/get-elected-get-your-kids-rich-washington-is-spoiled-rotten.html

27 ***Resilience:***
- American Psychological Association, The Road to Resilience http://www.apa.org/helpcenter/road-resilience.aspx
- Resilience – Building a World of Resilient Communities http://www.resilience.org/
- Transition Town Totnes "What is Resilience?" http://www.transitiontowntotnes.org/about/what-is-transition/what-is-resilience/
- What is Urban Resilience? (n.d.). Retrieved May 26, 2016, from http://www.100resilientcities.org/resilience#/-_Yz45MzIzNidpPTEocz5jbnBw/

28 ***Nixon:***
- Schultz, Colin, "Nixon Prolonged Vietnam War for Political Gain—And Johnson Knew About It, Newly Unclassified Tapes Suggest" Smart News,,Smithsonian March 18, 2013 http://www.smithsonianmag.com/smart-news/nixon-prolonged-vietnam-war-for-political-gainand-johnson-knew-about-it-newly-unclassified-tapes-suggest-3595441/#opSjQEcG1MsMyU0z.99

PAGE	RESOURCE

31   *Clinton*:
- Kounang, Nadia, "Big Pharma's Big Donations to 2016 Presidential Candidates", (Feb 11, 2016), CNN, http://www.cnn.com/2016/02/11/health/big-pharma-presidential-politics/
- Sirota, D. (2016, January 30). Hillary Clinton Gets $13 Million From Health Industry, Now Says Single-Payer Will. Retrieved May 19, 2016, from http://www.ibtimes.com/political-capital/hillary-clinton-gets-13-million-health-industry-now-says-single-payer-will-never

33   *Cruz:*
- Engel, P. (2015, December 19). Experts are casting doubt on Ted Cruz's strategy of 'carpet bombing' ISIS 'into oblivion' Retrieved May 19, 2016, from http://www.businessinsider.com/why-carpet-bombing-isis-wont-work-2015-12
- Agrawal, Nadya "Ted Cruz Sincles Out Anti-Abortion Groups In Flint For Water Donations" (Jan 25, 2016), Huffington Post: http://www.huffingtonpost.com/entry/ted-cruz-flint-water-abortion_us_56a649b4e4b0404eb8f23abb

34   *Deaths by Terrorism:*
- Qiu, Linda "Fact-checking a comparison of gun deaths and terrorism deaths" Oct 5th, 2015, Politifact: http://www.politifact.com/truth-o-meter/statements/2015/oct/05/viral-image/fact-checking-comparison-gun-deaths-and-terrorism-/

36   *FDR:*
- Franklin D. Roosevelt Presidential Library and Museum Interactive Periodic Table of the New Deal: http://www.fdrlibrary.marist.edu/education/resources/periodictable.html

PAGE   **RESOURCE**

39   ***Healthcare***
        • Health at a Glance 2015 – How does the United States
          compare? OECD – Organization for Economic Co-
          operation and Development:
          http://www.oecd.org/unitedstates/Health-at-a-Glance-
          2015-Key-Findings-UNITED-STATES.pdf
        • 2015 International Profiles of Health Care Systems, Jan
          2016, Edited by Elias Mossialos and Martin Wenzl –
          London School of Economics and Political Science and
          Robin Osborn and Dana Sarnak – The Commonwealth
          Fund:
          http://www.commonwealthfund.org/~/media/files/publicat
          ions/fund-
          report/2016/jan/1857_mossialos_intl_profiles_2015_v7.
          pdf?la=en
        • The Commonwealth Fund:
          http://www.commonwealthfund.org/
        • The Commonwealth Fund - Infographics of Surveys and
          Data:
          http://www.commonwealthfund.org/interactives-and-
          data/infographics
        • The Commonwealth Fund, Aiming Higher: Results from
          a Scorecard on State Health System Performance, 2015
          Edition. (n.d.). Retrieved May 19, 2016, from
          http://www.commonwealthfund.org/publications/fund-
          reports/2015/dec/aiming-higher-2015
        • Squires, David and Anderson, Chloe, "The
          Commonwealth Fund, Issues in International Health
          Policy – US Health Care from a Global Perspective:
          Spending, Use of Services, Prices, and Health in 13
          Countries":
          http://www.commonwealthfund.org/~/media/files/publicat
          ions/issue-
          brief/2015/oct/1819_squires_us_hlt_care_global_perspe
          ctive_oecd_intl_brief_v3.pdf
        •

PAGE	RESOURCE

40   ***Flint:***
- Wikipedia on the Flint Water Crisis: https://en.wikipedia.org/wiki/Flint_water_crisis
- New York Times, compilation of Flint articles "Events That Led to Flint's Water Crisis": http://www.nytimes.com/interactive/2016/01/21/us/flint-lead-water-timeline.html?_r=0

The ACLU documentary on Flint:
- Here's To Flint: Documentary on Flint Water Crisis | ACLU of Michigan. (Mar 8, 2016). Retrieved May 19, 2016, from http://www.aclumich.org/herestoflint

43   ***Carter:***
- Meadows, Donella. (n.d.). Dancing With Systems. Retrieved May 19, 2016, from http://www.donellameadows.org/archives/dancing-with-systems/ . *Used with permission.*

46   ***Arms***
- World's Top 5 arms exporters - Photos. (2015, November 17). Retrieved May 19, 2016, from http://www.upi.com/News_Photos/Features/Worlds-Top-5-arms-exporters/3105/

48   ***Eisenhower:***
- Dwight D. Eisenhower Quotes. (n.d.). Retrieved May 19, 2016, from https://www.goodreads.com/author/quotes/23920.Dwight_D_Eisenhower

49   ***Reagan:***
- Wold, N. (2015, January 15). 10 Reprehensible Crimes Of Ronald Reagan - Listverse. Retrieved May 19, 2016, from http://listverse.com/2015/01/15/10-reprehensible-crimes-of-ronald-reagan/

51   ***Bea Jackson*** http://beagifted.com/

53   ***Bradford Veley:*** brad@bradveley.com
More on Consumerism: The State of Consumption Today. (n.d.). Retrieved May 19, 2016, from http://www.worldwatch.org/node/810

54   ***Oklahoma Earthquakes:*** Oklahoma Geological Survey Get the data: http://earthquakes.ok.gov/

PAGE	RESOURCE

55   ***Plastic in the Oceans:***
- The Plastics Breakdown. (n.d.). Retrieved May 20, 2016, from http://www.oneworldoneocean.com/initiatives/PlasticsBreakdown
- The World of Knowledge: Agony caused plastic thrown into Sea: Turtle writhes in pain as drinking straw is pulled from its Nose. (n.d.). Retrieved May 20, 2016, from http://www.ilknowledge.com/2016/03/agony-caused-plastic-thrown-into-sea.html
- M. (2015, June 30). 20 Haunting Photos Of Environmental Pollution. Retrieved May 20, 2016, from http://www.pressroomvip.com/g/20-haunting-photos-of-environmental-pollution/
- Malik, W. (2016, March 31). Sperm Whales Found Full of Car Parts and Plastics. Retrieved May 20, 2016, from http://news.nationalgeographic.com/2016/03/160331-car-parts-plastics-dead-whales-germany-animals

56   ***Slave to Fashion:*** Minney, S. (n.d.). Slave to fashion. Retrieved May 20, 2016, from http://safia-minney.com/slave-to-fashion.html

57-60   ***Systems Tools and Systems Thinking Explained***
- Finding Leverage – The Power of Systems Thinking with Chris Soderquist. (n.d.). Retrieved May 20, 2016, from https://vimeo.com/113447134
- Predator Prey Dynamics – XMILE: http://www.iseesystems.com/XMILE/index.php?route=product/product&path=59&product_id=58
- XMILE Xchange: http://www.iseesystems.com/XMILE/
- **Waters Foundation**: Habits of a Systems Thinker - Waters Foundation. (n.d.). Retrieved May 20, 2016, from http://watersfoundation.org/systems-thinking/habits-of-a-systems-thinker/
- ***City Design:*** Cathcart-Keays, Athlyn and Warin, Tim. (2016, May 05). Story of cities #36: How Copenhagen rejected 1960s modernist 'utopia' Retrieved May 20, 2016, from http://www.theguardian.com/cities/2016/may/05/story-cities-copenhagen-denmark-modernist-utopia

PAGE	RESOURCE

57-60 • ***Trophic Cascade***: How Wolves Change Rivers - Sustainable Human. (2014, February 17). Retrieved May 20, 2016, from http://sustainablehuman.com/how-wolves-change-rivers/

61 ***Planetary Boundaries and Tipping Points***:
• Planetary boundaries. (n.d.). Retrieved May 20, 2016, from https://en.wikipedia.org/wiki/Planetary_boundaries
• Carey, J. (2015, March 05). The 9 limits of our planet ... and how we've raced past 4 of them. Retrieved May 20, 2016, from http://ideas.ted.com/the-9-limits-of-our-planet-and-how-weve-raced-past-4-of-them/
• Footprint Basics. (n.d.). Retrieved May 20, 2016, from http://www.footprintnetwork.org/en/index.php/GFN/page/footprint_basics_overview/ /

62 ***USA ranking on Environmental Issues:***
• Environmental Performance Index - Development. (n.d.). Retrieved May 20, 2016, from http://epi.yale.edu/chapter/key-findings
• Environmental Performance Index - Development. (n.d.). Retrieved May 20, 2016, from http://epi.yale.edu and http://epi.yale.edu/downloads
• Environmental Performance Index - USA. (2016 Report). Retrieved May 20, 2016, from http://epi.yale.edu/country/united-states-america
• Herzog, K. (2016, January 25). The United States ranks pathetically low on list of greenest nations. Retrieved May 20, 2016, from http://grist.org/article/the-united-states-ranks-pathetically-low-on-list-of-greenest-nations

63 ***World Wildlife Reports***:
• Half of Global Wildlife Lost, says new WWF Report. (2014, September 30). Retrieved May 20, 2016, from http://www.worldwildlife.org/press-releases/half-of-global-wildlife-lost-says-new-wwf-report
• Living Planet Report 2014. (2014, September 30). Retrieved May 20, 2016, from http://www.worldwildlife.org/publications/living-planet-report-2014

PAGE	RESOURCE

66   ***Waste in Government:***
- Fragmentation, Overlap, and Duplication: An Evaluation and Management Guide. (n.d.). Retrieved May 20, 2016, from http://www.gao.gov/products/GAO-15-49SP and http://www.gao.gov/assets/670/669365.pdf
- U.S. GAO - Fragmentation, Overlap, and Duplication: An Evaluation and Management Guide. (n.d.). Retrieved May 20, 2016, from http://gao.gov/framework_duplication/overview
- All Reports-Office of Inspector General | oig.state.gov. (n.d.). Retrieved May 20, 2016, from https://oig.state.gov/reports
- SEMIANNUAL REPORT TO THE CONGRESS - oig.state.gov. (n.d.). Retrieved May 20, 2016, from https://oig.state.gov/system/files/oig_fall_2015_sar.pdf
- Performance measurement. (n.d.). Retrieved May 20, 2016, from https://en.wikipedia.org/wiki/Performance_measurement

67   ***Linear vs Circular – three system cycles:***
- **Biomimicry**: Biomimicry 3.8. (n.d.). Retrieved May 20, 2016, from http://biomimicry.net/

   Making it FUN:
- The Fun Theory. (n.d.). Retrieved May 20, 2016, from http://www.thefuntheory.com/
- **Piano Stairs**: The Fun Theory. (n.d.). Retrieved May 20, 2016, from http://www.thefuntheory.com/piano-staircase
- **Bottle Arcade**: The Fun Theory. (n.d.). Retrieved May 20, 2016, from http://www.thefuntheory.com/bottle-bank-arcade-machine
- **Deepest Bin**: The Fun Theory. (n.d.). Retrieved May 20, 2016, from http://www.thefuntheory.com/worlds-deepest-bin

PAGE	RESOURCE

67-68 ***Circular Economy:***
- Circular Economy System Diagram - Ellen MacArthur Foundation. (n.d.). Retrieved May 20, 2016, from https://www.ellenmacarthurfoundation.org/circular-economy/interactive-diagram Circular Economy - UK, Europe, Asia, South America & USA | Ellen MacArthur Foundation. (n.d.). Retrieved May 20, 2016, from https://www.ellenmacarthurfoundation.org/circular-economy

69 ***Biomimicry:***
- Biomimicry 3.8. (n.d.). Retrieved May 20, 2016, from http://biomimicry.net/
- Biomimicry Design Toolbox. (n.d.). Retrieved May 20, 2016, from http://toolbox.biomimicry.org/ _,
- Ask Nature: How does nature... (n.d.). Retrieved May 20, 2016, from http://www.asknature.org/

70 ***Biomimicry Examples:***
- Sharklet Technologies, Inc. (n.d.). Retrieved May 20, 2016, from: http://sharklet.com/
- The Future of Bird-Friendly Architecture is Clear... (n.d.). Retrieved May 20, 2016, from http://www.ornilux.com/

71-72 ***Environmental Accountability -***
- Koronowski, R. (2014, January 30). The Extraordinary Climate And Environmental Legacy Of Henry Waxman. Retrieved May 20, 2016, from http://thinkprogress.org/climate/2014/01/30/3228001/waxman-climate-legacy/
- Top Five Eco-Friendly Politicians of 2013. (2013, December 12). Retrieved May 20, 2016, from http://www.postconsumers.com/education/best-politicians-2013/
- Grist Staff, 15 Green Politicians. (2007, June 27). Retrieved May 20, 2016, from http://grist.org/article/politicians/

PAGE	RESOURCE

72 ***Environmental Accountability – More:***

- Mayors Climate Protection Center: The Agreement. (n.d.). Retrieved May 20, 2016, from http://www.usmayors.org/climateprotection/ClimateChange.asp
- Phillips, Ari. (2014, June 22). Mayors Sign Climate Protection Agreement, Endorse Innovative Climate Solutions. Retrieved May 20, 2016, from http://thinkprogress.org/climate/2014/06/22/3451702/mayors-conference-climate-change/
- The Daily Beast Staff, (n.d.). "America's Greenest Politicians From Barbara Boxer to John Kerry" Retrieved May 20, 2016, from http://www.thedailybeast.com/galleries/2012/10/18/america-s-greenest-politicians-from-barbara-boxer-to-john-kerry.html
- Schroeder, J. (2014, June 25). U.S. Mayors Expand Climate Protection Agreement. Retrieved May 20, 2016, from http://energy.agwired.com/2014/06/25/u-s-mayors-expand-climate-protection-agreement/
- The U.S. Conference of Mayors 82nd Annual Meeting June 20 .Resolutions Proposed.. (n.d.). Retrieved May 20, 2016, from http://www.usmayors.org/82ndAnnualMeeting/media/resolutions-proposed.pdf

73 ***Chris Gibson's (R-NY) Resolution (H. Res 424):***

- Bill Widget for H.Res. 424. (2015, September 17). Retrieved May 20, 2016, from https://www.govtrack.us/congress/bills/114/hres424/widget
- Tell your Republican member of Congress you support the Gibson Climate Change Resolution! (n.d.). Retrieved May 20, 2016, from https://citizensclimatelobby.org/gibson-climate-change-resolution/
- Gibson, C. (2015, September 17). Environmental Stewardship Resolution - Chris Gibson. Retrieved May 20, 2016, from http://gibson.house.gov/uploadedfiles/environmental_stewardship_resolution.pdf

PAGE	RESOURCE

74 **Anti-Science Homo Politicanus:**
- McCarthy, T. (2014, November 17). Meet the Republicans in Congress who don't believe climate change is real. Retrieved May 21, 2016, from http://www.theguardian.com/environment/2014/nov/17/climate-change-denial-scepticism-republicans-congress
- From the Pew Research Center: Gewurz, D. (2013, November 01). GOP Deeply Divided Over Climate Change. Retrieved May 21, 2016, from http://www.people-press.org/2013/11/01/gop-deeply-divided-over-climate-change/
- Check out the 2015 National Environmental Scorecard. (n.d.). Retrieved May 21, 2016, from http://scorecard.lcv.org/?p=c
- All Member of Congress Scores. (n.d.). Retrieved May 21, 2016, from http://scorecard.lcv.org/members-of-congress
- Scorecards - Washington Conservation Voters. (n.d.). Retrieved May 21, 2016, from https://wcvoters.org/our-work/scorecard/

When adults fail, sometimes CHILDREN LEAD THE WAY:
- Youths Secure Second Win In ... - Our Children's Trust. (2016, April 29). Retrieved May 21, 2016, from http://ourchildrenstrust.org/sites/default/files/2016.04.29WAFinalRulingPR.pdf
- The Children's Climate Crusade: Legal Action. (n.d.). Retrieved May 21, 2016, from http://ourchildrenstrust.org/Legal

77-78 **Edge Effect:**
- Permaculture Design Principles. (n.d.). Retrieved May 21, 2016, from https://permacultureprinciples.com/principles/
- Drawing inspired by:: *Bart Johnson, Kristina Hill – "Ecology and Design, Frameworks for Learning", Island Press, 2002*
- 10. Edge Effect. (2013). Retrieved May 21, 2016, from https://deepgreenpermaculture.com/permaculture/permaculture-design-principles/10-edge-effect/

PAGE	RESOURCE

79 *Precautionary Principle:*

- Science & Environmental Health Network - Precautionary Principle. (n.d.). Retrieved May 21, 2016, from http://www.sehn.org/precaution.html
- The European Union Law on the Precautionary Principle: EUR-Lex Access to European Union law. (n.d.). Retrieved May 21, 2016, from http://eur-lex.europa.eu/legal-content/EN/TXT/?uri=URISERV:l21170 and from the Glossary of Summaries: Precautionary Principle: http://eur-lex.europa.eu/summary/glossary/precautionary_principl e.html
- EXAMPLE: Bush, Ashley, Holsinger Jr, J, and Prybil, L.. (2016, February 4). Employing the Precautionary Principle to Evaluate the Use of E-Cigarettes. Retrieved May 21, 2016, from http://journal.frontiersin.org/article/10.3389/fpubh.2016.0 0005/full

80 *No willingness to embrace diversity:*

- S.C. Lawmaker Refers to Obama and Nikki Haley as "Raghead" (2010, June 4). Retrieved May 21, 2016, from http://www.cbsnews.com/news/sc-lawmaker-refers-to-obama-and-nikki-haley-as-raghead

81 *Willingness to embrace diversity:*

- Shipps, J. (2015, July 5). 'You have to be honest:' Michael Steele schools the Republican Party about racism. Retrieved May 21, 2016, from http://www.rawstory.com/2015/07/you-have-to-be-honest-michael-steele-schools-the-republican-party-about-racism/
- Another point of view worth considering: Ea, P. (2015, November 2). I Am NOT Black, You are NOT White. Retrieved May 21, 2016, from https://youtu.be/q0qD2K2RWkc

PAGE	RESOURCE

82   *Willingness to embrace diverse people. Example, regarding Refugees:*
- What you need to know: Crisis in Syria, refugees, and the impact on children. (2016, May 11). Retrieved May 21, 2016, from https://www.worldvision.org/wv/news/Syria-war-refugee-crisis-FAQ

84   *National Economic Health: GDP/GNP/GPI:*
- **GDP/GNP**: InvestorWords.com - Online Investing Glossary. (n.d.). Retrieved May 21, 2016, from http://www.investorwords.com/article/gdp-vs-gnp.html
- **GDP/GNP**: Milton, C. (2008). GPI: A Preferable Metric To GDP? Retrieved May 21, 2016, from http://inspiredeconomist.com/2008/10/16/gdp-vs-gpi-which-measures-the-economy-best/
- **GDP/GNP**: Gross Domestic Product (GDP) vs Gross National Product (GNP). (n.d.). Retrieved May 21, 2016, from http://www.diffen.com/difference/GDP_vs_GNP
- **GDP/GPI**: Differences Between GDP and GPI. (2012). Retrieved May 21, 2016, from http://www.differencebetween.net/business/economics-business/differences-between-gdp-and-gpi/
- **GPI**: Talberth, J. Cobb, C. Slattery, N The Genuine Progress Indicator 2006 – A Tool for Sustainable Development. Retrieved May 21, 2016, from Redefining Progress – The Nature of Economics: http://rprogress.org/publications/2007/GPI%202006.pdf
- **GPI**: Genuine progress indicator. (n.d.). Retrieved May 21, 2016, from Wikipedia: https://en.wikipedia.org/wiki/Genuine_progress_indicator
- **GPI**: ReDefining Progress: Genuine Progress Indicator. (n.d.). Retrieved May 21, 2016, from http://rprogress.org/sustainability_indicators/genuine_progress_indicator.htm
- Cooney, S. (2013). Sustainable Economics: Tim Jackson gives a reality check. Retrieved May 21, 2016, from http://inspiredeconomist.com/2013/08/07/sustainable-economics-tim-jackson-gives-a-reality-check/

PAGE	RESOURCE

85   *Inequality Metrics: Gini/Palma/IHDI...*

- Stokel-Walker, C. (2015, March 12). Who, What, Why: What is the Gini coefficient? Retrieved May 21, 2016, from http://www.bbc.com/news/blogs-magazine-monitor-31847943
- COUNTRY COMPARISON :: DISTRIBUTION OF FAMILY INCOME - GINI INDEX. (n.d.). Retrieved May 21, 2016, from https://www.cia.gov/library/publications/resources/the-world-factbook/rankorder/2172rank.html
- **Palma vs Gini**: Cobham, A. (2013, April 5). Palma vs Gini: Measuring post-2015 inequality. Retrieved May 21, 2016, from http://www.cgdev.org/blog/palma-vs-gini-measuring-post-2015-inequality
- **Gini**: GINI index (World Bank estimate). (n.d.). Retrieved May 21, 2016, from http://data.worldbank.org/indicator/SI.POV.GINI
- **Gini**: Kiersz, A. (2014, November 08). Here Are The Most Unequal Countries In The World. Retrieved May 21, 2016, from http://www.businessinsider.com/gini-index-income-inequality-world-map-2014-11
- Sherman, E. (2015, September 29). America is the richest, and most unequal, country. Retrieved May 21, 2016, from http://fortune.com/2015/09/30/america-wealth-inequality

Wealth and Inequality continued ...

- Fisher, M. (2013, September 27). Map: How the world's countries compare on income inequality (the U.S. ranks below Nigeria). Retrieved May 21, 2016, from https://www.washingtonpost.com/news/worldviews/wp/2013/09/27/map-how-the-worlds-countries-compare-on-income-inequality-the-u-s-ranks-below-nigeria/
- **Oxfam 2015 Report on Corporate & Elite Influence:** https://www.oxfam.org/sites/www.oxfam.org/files/file_attachments/ib-wealth-having-all-wanting-more-190115-en.pdf

PAGE	RESOURCE

85 cont.

Trickle-down Theory:
- Keller, J. (2015, June 18). The IMF Confirms That 'Trickle-Down' Economics Is, Indeed, a Joke - Pacific Standard. Retrieved May 21, 2016, from https://psmag.com/the-imf-confirms-that-trickle-down-economics-is-indeed-a-joke-207d7ca469b#.hj8n2skqd

OECD and other indices:
- Income Distribution and Poverty. (n.d.). Retrieved May 21, 2016, from https://stats.oecd.org/Index.aspx?DataSetCode=IDD
- Gbadamosi, A. (n.d.). Understanding international indices of inequality. Retrieved May 21, 2016, from http://www.a4id.org/blog/understanding-international-indices-inequality

United Nations - Inequality-Adjusted Human Development Index (IHDI)
- Human Development Reports. (2015). Retrieved May 21, 2016, from http://hdr.undp.org/en/content/inequality-adjusted-human-development-index-ihdi
- UNITED NATIONS DEVELOPMENT PROGRAMME Human Development Reports - USA. (n.d.). Retrieved May 21, 2016, from http://www.hdr.undp.org/en/countries/profiles/USA
- Human Development Reports 2015 - Web Version. (n.d.). Retrieved May 21, 2016, from http://hdr.undp.org/en/2014-report
- Human Development Reports - FAQ Page - IHDI. (n.d.). Retrieved May 21, 2016, from http://hdr.undp.org/en/faq-page/inequality-adjusted-human-development-index-ihdi

Gilens and Page findings:
- Gilens, M., Page, Benjamin I. (2014, September 18). Testing Theories of American Politics: Elites, Interest Groups, and Average Citizens. - Retrieved May 21, 2016, from http://journals.cambridge.org/action/displayAbstract?aid=9354310

PAGE	RESOURCE

87 **Various Forms of Capital and Currency:**
- Hoffer, D. and Levy, M. (n.d.). Measuring Community Wealth - yellowwood.org. Retrieved May 23, 2016, from http://www.yellowwood.org/assets/resource_library/res ource_docs/measuringcommunitywealth.pdf
- Roland, E and Landua, G. (2011, April). 8 Forms of Capital | AppleSeed Permaculture. Retrieved May 23, 2016, from http://www.appleseedpermaculture.com/8-forms-of-capital/
- Ellis, B. (2012, January). Funny money? 11 local currencies. Retrieved May 23, 2016, from http://money.cnn.com/galleries/2012/pf/1201/gallery.co mmunity-currencies/7.html
- Complementary Currency Resource Center. (n.d.). Retrieved May 23, 2016, from http://complementarycurrency.org/
- LETS - Local Exchange Trading Systems. (n.d.). Retrieved May 23, 2016, from http://www.transaction.net/money/lets/
- We Need Each Other. (n.d.). Retrieved May 23, 2016, from http://timebanks.org/
- Economic Crisis Currency Strategies and Solutions. (n.d.). Retrieved May 23, 2016, from http://www.lietaer.com/

90 **Quality of Life Indicators:**
- How's life? OECD (n.d.). Retrieved May 23, 2016, from http://www.oecdbetterlifeindex.org/
- Quality of Life in the cities of the Urban Audit. (2014). Retrieved May 23, 2016, from http://www.bfs.admin.ch/bfs/portal/en/index/internation al/03/04/07.html
- Balancing paid work, unpaid work and leisure. (2014, July 3). Retrieved May 23, 2016, from https://www.oecd.org/gender/data/balancingpaidworku npaidworkandleisure.htm

PAGE	RESOURCE

90
cont.

Quality of Life Indicators continued:
- Work-Life Balance. (n.d.). Retrieved May 23, 2016, from http://www.oecdbetterlifeindex.org/topics/work-life-balance/
- Additional excellent analysis of global converging cultural values and their political trends can be found here: WVS Database. (n.d.). Retrieved May 23, 2016, from http://www.worldvaluessurvey.org/WVSContents.jsp

92

Denmark's Business Model and Capitalism:
- Forbes: . (2015, December 17). Retrieved May 23, 2016, from http://www.investindk.com/News-and-events/News/2015/Forbes-Denmark-Worlds-Best-Country-for-Business

Opportunity to get rich: TED Talk -
Eia, H. (2016, May 2). Where in the world is it easiest to get rich? | Harald Eia | TEDxOslo. Retrieved May 23, 2016, from https://youtu.be/A9UmdY0E8hU

Where Capitalism Breaks Down...
- Cooney, S. (2012). Where conservative capitalism breaks down: Three primary sources of free market failure - The Inspired Economist. Retrieved May 23, 2016, from http://inspiredeconomist.com/2012/09/07/where-conservative-capitalism-breaks-downthree-primary-sources-of-free-market-failure/

World's Happiest Countries:
- Pullella, P. (2016, March 15). This Is The World's Happiest Country - from Reuters. Fortune Magazine Retrieved May 23, 2016, from http://fortune.com/2016/03/16/worlds-happiest-country/
- Helliwell, J., Layard, R., & Sachs, J. (2016). *World Happiness Report 2016, Update (Vol. I)*. New York: Sustainable Development Solutions Network http://worldhappiness.report/ed/2016/
- World Happiness Report 2016 Update Ranks Happiest Countries. (2016, March 16). Retrieved May 23, 2016, from http://unsdsn.org/news/2016/03/16/world-happiness-report-2016-update-ranks-happiest-countries/

PAGE	RESOURCE

94   ***Gov. Rick Scott:***
- Sherman, A. (2014, March 3). Rick Scott 'oversaw the largest Medicare fraud' in U.S. history, Florida Democratic Party says. Retrieved May 23, 2016, from http://www.politifact.com/florida/statements/2014/mar/03/florida-democratic-party/rick-scott-rick-scott-oversaw-largest-medicare-fra/

The Panama Papers:
- The Panama Papers - The International Consortium of Investigative Journalists - The Center for Public Integrity. (n.d.). Retrieved May 23, 2016, from https://panamapapers.icij.org/

IMF: Inequality - A Global Perspective
- Dabla-Norris, E. Kochhar, K., Suphaphiphat, N., Ricka, F., Tsounta, E. "Causes and Consequences of Income Inequality: A Global Perspective" Retrieved May 23, 2016 from: https://www.imf.org/external/pubs/ft/sdn/2015/sdn1513.pdf

96   ***US Constitution***
- The Constitution of the United States: A Transcription, Retrieved May 23, 2016 from: http://www.archives.gov/exhibits/charters/constitution_transcript.html

Second Amendment:
- Toobin, J. (2012, December 17). So You Think You Know the Second Amendment? Retrieved May 23, 2016, from http://www.newyorker.com/news/daily-comment/so-you-think-you-know-the-second-amendment
- Second Amendment - Cornell University Law School. (n.d.). Retrieved May 23, 2016, from https://www.law.cornell.edu/wex/second_amendment

96
cont.

US Constitution continued...
  Second Amendment continued...
* Waldman, M. (2014, June 19). The Second Amendment doesn't say what you think it does. Retrieved May 23, 2016, from http://www.motherjones.com/politics/2014/06/second-amendment-guns-michael-waldman

How many in USA killed by terrorists?
* LaCapria, K. (2015, December 17). TRUE: More Americans Killed by Toddlers than Terrorists. Retrieved May 23, 2016, from http://www.snopes.com/toddlers-killed-americans-terrorists/

98

Restrictive Voter Laws:
* Voting Laws Roundup 2015 | Brennan Center for Justice. (2015, June 3). Retrieved May 23, 2016, from https://www.brennancenter.org/analysis/voting-laws-roundup-2015
* New Voting Restrictions in Place for 2016 Presidential Election | Brennan Center for Justice. (2016, April 4). Retrieved May 23, 2016, from http://www.brennancenter.org/voting-restrictions-first-time-2016
* Sensenbrenner Jr. [R-WI-5], R.. (Introduced Feb 11, 2015). All Info - H.R.885 - 114th Congress (2015-2016): Voting Rights Amendment Act of 2015. Retrieved May 23, 2016, from https://www.congress.gov/bill/114th-congress/house-bill/885/all-info
* Sensenbrenner, J. (2016, March 31). Suppress Votes? I'd Rather Lose My Job. Retrieved May 23, 2016, from http://www.nytimes.com/2016/03/31/opinion/suppress-votes-id-rather-lose-my-job.html?_r=0

PAGE	RESOURCE

99   *Voter Fraud:*

- Bump, P. (2014, October 13). The disconnect between voter ID laws and voter fraud. Retrieved May 23, 2016, from https://www.washingtonpost.com/news/the-fix/wp/2014/10/13/the-disconnect-between-voter-id-laws-and-voter-fraud/
- Levitt, J. (2014, August 6). A comprehensive investigation of voter impersonation finds 31 credible incidents out of one billion ballots cast. Retrieved May 23, 2016, from https://www.washingtonpost.com/news/wonk/wp/2014/08/06/a-comprehensive-investigation-of-voter-impersonation-finds-31-credible-incidents-out-of-one-billion-ballots-cast/
- Restricting the Vote | Brennan Center for Justice - New York University School of Law. (n.d.). Retrieved May 23, 2016, from https://www.brennancenter.org/issues/restricting-vote
- US Court of Appeals for the 7t Circuit – Nos. 14-2058 & 14-2059, (2014, October 10). Retrieved May 23, 2016, from https://s3.amazonaws.com/s3.documentcloud.org/documents/1312285/posner.pdf
- Sobel, R., (2014, June), Harvard Law School Institute for Race & Justice, "The High Cost of 'Free' Photo Voter Identification Cards", Retrieved May 23, 2016 from: http://www.charleshamiltonhouston.org/wp-content/uploads/2014/08/FullReportVoterIDJune2014.pdf

100   *Elected Officials' Voter Fraud:*

- Mouse, N. (2012, November 20). If Politicians Wanted To End Voter Fraud, They'd Clean House. Retrieved May 23, 2016, from http://crooksandliars.com/nonny-mouse/if-politicians-really-wanted-stamp-out

PAGE	RESOURCE

100 **_Elected Officials' Voter Fraud_** _continued..._
Cont.
- Levin, M. (2016, February 15). **'Last Week Tonight'** recalls Houston lawmaker's hypocrisy in Texas voter ID laws. Retrieved May 23, 2016, from http://www.chron.com/news/politics/article/Last-Week-Tonight-points-out-hypocrisy-in-6831726.php

101 **_Electoral College issues:_**
- Greer, C. (2012, November 1). Does your vote count? The Electoral College explained - Christina Greer., TED Ed, Retrieved May 23, 2016, from http://ed.ted.com/lessons/does-your-vote-count-the-electoral-college-explained-christina-greer#review
- Jackson, B. (2008, January 22). The Florida Recount of 2000. Retrieved May 23, 2016, from http://www.factcheck.org/2008/01/the-florida-recount-of-2000/

102 **_Instant Runoff Voting & Ranked Choice Voting:_**
- Frequently Asked Questions. (n.d.). Retrieved May 23, 2016, from https://www.acgov.org/rov/rcv/faq.htm
- Ranked Choice Voting / Instant Runoff- FairVote. (n.d.). Retrieved May 23, 2016, from http://www.fairvote.org/rcv#rcvbenefits

103- **_Democracy Rankings Worldwide:_**
104
- Atlee, T. (n.d.). The Co-Intelligence Institute. http://www.co-intelligence.org/
- Democracy Ranking 2015. (n.d.). Retrieved May 24, 2016, from http://democracyranking.org/wordpress/rank/democracy-ranking -2015
- Democracy Index 2015: Democracy in an age of anxiety. (n.d.). Retrieved May 24, 2016, from http://www.eiu.com/public/topical_report.aspx?campaignid=DemocracyIndex2015
- Democracy Index 2014. (n.d.). Retrieved May 24, 2016, from https://www.eiu.com/public/topical_report.aspx?campaignid=Democracy0115
  - o

PAGE	RESOURCE

105   *Separation of Church and State:*
- Glueck, K. (2016, January 20). Cruz: 'Washington establishment' backs Drumpf, has abandoned Rubio. Retrieved May 24, 2016, from http://www.politico.com/story/2016/01/ted-cruz-establishment-trump-rubio-218047
- Boston, R. (2015, November 13). Wall of Separation. Retrieved May 24, 2016, from https://www.au.org/blogs/wall-of-separation/on-your-knees-cruz-insists-that-good-leaders-need-god
- **Cruz scores** 100% by Americans United for the Separation of Church and State
  Scoring system for 2014: Ranges from:
  - **0%** (supports separation of church & state) to
  - **100%** (opposed to separation of church & state).
  - Home | Americans United for Separation of Church and State. (n.d.). https://www.au.org
- Cruz renounced Canadian citizenship May 14, 2014, over a year after becoming a US Senator. Wofford, T. (2016, January 13). Retrieved May 24, 2016, from http://www.newsweek.com/ted-cruz-canadian-citizen-415430

107   *Equality and Equity:*
- Difference Between Equity and Equality. (2010). Retrieved May 24, 2016, from http://www.differencebetween.net/language/difference-between-equity-and-equality/

110   *Torture and "Enhanced Interrogation"*
- CIA tactics: What is 'enhanced interrogation'? (2014, December 10). Retrieved May 24, 2016, from http://www.bbc.com/news/world-us-canada-11723189
- Winsor, M. (2014, December 12). Why Did The CIA Torture When They Knew Interrogation Techniques Didn't Work? Senate Report Shows History Repeats Itself. Retrieved May 24, 2016, from http://www.ibtimes.com/why-did-cia-torture-when-they-knew-interrogation-techniques-didnt-work-senate-report-1746718

PAGE	RESOURCE

119
Cont.

Quality Communication:
Nonviolent Communication: continued …
- Rosenberg, M. (n.d.). Marshall Rosenberg's NVC Quote Collection. Retrieved May 24, 2016, from http://www.nonviolentcommunication.com/freeresources/nvc_social_media_quotes.htm

Historical perspective on nonviolence:
- Global Nonviolent Action Database. (n.d.). Retrieved May 24, 2016, from http://nvdatabase.swarthmore.edu/

121-
122

Better Storytelling:
- Krasley, S. (2012, July 3). How Nora Ephron's Films Can Teach Sustainability Entrepreneurs To Tell Better Stories. Retrieved May 24, 2016, from http://www.fastcoexist.com/1680130/how-nora-ephrons-films-can-teach-sustainability-entrepreneurs-to-tell-better-stories

Storytelling with Chris Soderquist
- Soderquist, C. (2015). Finding Leverage – The Power of Systems Thinking with Chris Soderquist. Retrieved May 24, 2016, from https://vimeo.com/113447134
- Soderquist, C. (2010, April 29). We have met an ally and he is Storytelling. Retrieved May 24, 2016, from http://blog.iseesystems.com/systems-thinking/we-have-met-an-ally-and-he-is-storytelling/
- Soderquist, C. (n.d.). Forio Simulate - We have met an ally and he is Storytelling. Retrieved May 24, 2016, from https://forio.com/simulate/pontifexconsult/response-to-ny-times/overview/

How to motivate others toward change:
- Stillman, J. (2016, March 18). A Stanford Psychologist Explains How to Motivate Others to Change. Retrieved May 24, 2016, from http://www.inc.com/jessica-stillman/how-to-motivate-others-to-change.html
- 50 Per Cent More Motivation With This Way of Thinking About Rewards - PsyBlog. (2016, February 17). Retrieved May 24, 2016, from http://www.spring.org.uk/2016/02/reward-versus-loss.php

PAGE	RESOURCE

122 cont. *How to motivate others toward change, continued...*
- Patel, M. S. (2016, February 16). Framing Financial Incentives to Increase Physical Activity Among Overweight and Obese Adults: A Randomized, Controlled TrialFinancial Incentives for Physical Activity in Overweight and Obese Adults. Retrieved May 24, 2016, from http://annals.org/article.aspx?articleid=2491916
- Hostyn, J. (n.d.). Psychology of change. Retrieved May 24, 2016, from http://www.joycehostyn.com/blog/2012/05/16/psychology-of-change/
- Krasley, S. (2012, July 3). How Nora Ephron's Films Can Teach Sustainability Entrepreneurs To Tell Better Stories. Retrieved May 24, 2016, from http://www.fastcoexist.com/1680130/how-nora-ephrons-films-can-teach-sustainability-entrepreneurs-to-tell-better-stories

The Center for Compassion and Altruism Research and Education -
- The Center for Compassion and Altruism Research and Education (CCARE). (n.d.). Retrieved May 24, 2016, from http://ccare.stanford.edu/

Why we make the choices we do even irrational ones:
- Clear, J. (2016, March 18). Why We Act Irrationally: A Harvard Psychologist Reveals the One Word That Drives Our Senseless Habits. Retrieved May 24, 2016, from http://www.huffingtonpost.com/james-clear/why-we-act-irrationally-a_b_9478748.html

To better understand change states and complexity of thinking:
- Spiral dynamics ® | NVC Consulting – Spiral Dynamics® Training & Graves Theory. (n.d.). Retrieved May 24, 2016, from http://spiraldynamics.org/

143 TransitionUS
- Welcome | Transition US. (n.d.). Retrieved May 24, 2016, from http://www.transitionus.org/
- Welcome to the Global Transition Network. (n.d.). Retrieved May 24, 2016, from https://www.transitionnetwork.org/

ABOUT THE AUTHOR

Shaktari Belew has been an observer of nature, artist, designer, author, and playful explorer all her life.

She was introduced to systems thinking in the COBOL/JCL days of computers, and applied it to every field she studied thereafter. International travel opened her eyes to cultural, social, and political variations. To her they are all experiments in action, each worthy of attention, as each offers valuable lessons for our species. Multiple fields of formal study and experience in work environments deepened and multiplied her questions as patterns emerged. And through teaching, she learned limits and creative methodologies.

Mom to three and grandma to one (so far), she has continually learned from them, and expanded her points-of-view as they stretched her to question her assumptions and beliefs. It is for them and all future generations that she explored new educational systems and developed several non-profits.

She was one of seven educators who combined the best of education worldwide to develop 4 pilot learner-led K-12 schools located in the USA and South Africa. That jump-started her awareness of the incredible work in all fields of human endeavor throughout the world that focused on life-enhancing, nature-honoring solutions. After almost 5 years of research, she published her findings in the 2005 book, *Honoring All Life*.

This led her to investigate how nature develops survival strategies and processes that are life-enhancing, like Biomimicry and Permaculture. In 2008, she had the pleasure of being chosen as one of the first *TransitionUS* workshop trainers, traveling throughout the USA exploring resilient community strategies within diverse communities and bio-regions.

These journeys have been incredibly educational. Most of all, she learned that whatever we do, making it FUN and creating the space for people to explore their passions and give their best, usually yields the best for everyone.

Made in the USA
San Bernardino, CA
13 July 2016